REV. DAFFA JAMMO AND I

The Reminiscence of Our Lives In My Own Words

First Edition

KANATU KARORSA

ISBN 978-1-0980-6886-8 (paperback)
ISBN 978-1-0980-6887-5 (digital)

Copyright © 2024 by Abby Daffa

All rights reserved. No part of this publication may be reproduced, distributed, or transmitted in any form or by any means, including photocopying, recording, or other electronic or mechanical methods without the prior written permission of the publisher. For permission requests, solicit the publisher via the address below.

Christian Faith Publishing
832 Park Avenue
Meadville, PA 16335
www.christianfaithpublishing.com

Printed in the United States of America

Mrs. Kanatu Karorsa and The Rev. Daffa Jammo

The Reminiscence of Our Lives
In My Own Words

Mrs. Kanatu Karorsa

Mrs. Kanatu Karorsa at age 97

CONTENTS

Abby's Note ix
Acknowledgments xv
1 General Portrait of Our Lives 1
2 My Early Life 4
3 Life Together 22
4 Looking for People Who Were Willing to Learn 30
5 What We Needed for Our Daily Life 35
6 "Come Over and Help Us": Nadjjoo, Boodjii,
   Mandii, and Naqamtee 39
7 Incidents on Trips 42
8 Move to Finfinnee for Training 45
9 From Finfinnee to Qaannao 48
10 Church in Waalgo Aira 51
11 The Return of the German Hermannsburg
   Missionaries to Aira 55
12 Expansion of the Work in Collaboration with the
   Missionaries 62
13 Formation of Gimbii Awraja Board (Later EECMY
   Western Synod) and Appointment as President 66
14 Life during Communist Turmoil 69
15 My hand crafts Work 75
16 Family and Friends 84
17 Legacy 102
18 Our Children 106
19 Humorous Short Stories 118
20 Retirement 122
21 Life after the Departure of My Husband 130

22	Accomplishments	134
23	Letters and Poems from Our Children	138
24	Notes from Our Godchildren Dr. Bichaka Fayissa and Ms. Aster Bato	150
25	Note from Dr. Harvey Doorenbos	156

ABBY'S NOTE

It has been a great pleasure to sit with my mother and listen to the story of my parents from before I was born and after. The beginning of their life together was hard for me to grasp compared to the story after I was born. I quickly connected with the story that I knew after my birth because I saw firsthand the walk they took and the hardships they endured.

By observing their lives, I learned a lifetime lesson that made me strong. I was astonished at how steadfast they were in their lives. They were blessed with the growth of Christian community and the fruit that was budding.

Before writing what I heard from her, I asked my mother if she wanted me to write a short story about her life. My siblings and I wanted something special to remember about our parents. Of course, close friends of our parents were always asking Mamma to write the story of their lives together. Hence, my mother wanted to pass their story on to someone who was interested to write it. She told me to write about the seventy-year story of their lives together and their work, and this could take over four to five volumes.

What follows is just a short documentary of their lives together in the service of our Lord Jesus Christ. She told me as much as she remembers, noting that some of the stories had been already written by the German Hermannsburg missionaries, in case anyone wants to get a more complete picture.

My sister Tsion is writing a biography of our father using our father's biography that he wrote and left behind for us before he passed away. This biography is not about his personal life but is only about church matters. He gave it out before to some of the pastors to let them know what he was about to publish. Our father died without publishing many of his books. I learned from my sister that part of the story was already taken out and published from those pastors, and she is going to verify those parts and publish them.

As our mother mentioned in her autobiography, our father had written so many books since the early 1950s on many subjects, such as the story of churches, Oromo cultural books, Kussa afaan Oromo (dictionary), Mamaksa Afaan Oromo (quotes), and Gerarsa Oromo (Oromo songs and poems). He translated spiritual songs from German to Afaan Oromo. He also wrote children's story books from which he narrated so many stories to us in the evening. We gathered around him as he taught us children's games around the fire area.

He emphasized the meaning of our Oromo names and taught us that Oromo people never named their children without any meaning. The name of a person must have a reason to be named. Some of these books were published, and the rest of them will be published in the near future.

He honored Onesimos's work and discussed his achievements extensively. He established the Onesimos Nesiib Seminary School in Aira Wollaga on his own land, with Pastor Ernst Bauerochse and Manfred Zach. These two pastors were our father's backbone. They worked hard with our father to enhance the work of Christianity in Western Wollaga and beyond. He was so grateful to have missionaries by his side to accomplish his dreams for his people. I know and believe that he was totally satisfied and nothing was left undone on his part. I am honored to be his daughter and proud of the achievements he made before he departed from this earth.

Loving father and Abby 1984

While telling my parents' story, I learned the special trait that carried them both through their rough journey to a solid, true Christian life. This trait extended through all circumstances: their wedding, the birth of their children, their deaths, incidences, character, honesty, respect, love, hardship, patience, humor, and destination. The trait is faith in God, who gave them the ability to stand firm for the work He entrusted to them.

Through this assignment, they honored, respected, and loved Him and carried out the promises they vowed. They cleared the rough road, and they were the stepping stones for many people to come to the knowledge of Jesus Christ as Lord and Savior. They completed their duties with respect and left nothing unfinished on their part. Their hearts' desires were fulfilled in Christ.

I believe that the day Wassmann took our mother's picture in Dambii Dolloo—without her knowledge at the age of fifteen to show it to our father—was the moment that God marked them for one another and made them His own instruments. Wassmann saw our mother when she was in the care of the American Presbyterian Mission in Dambii Dolloo, and he wanted her to be married to our father. Upon his return to Aira, Wassmann showed her picture to our father, Daffa Jammo, and our father agreed to marry her. They were true believers of Christ Jesus, and He is glorified through their humble journey together.

In this journey of their lives together, I know that the Good Lord rejoiced in the faith they had in Him and the effort they made to bring people to Christ. They won lost souls, planted churches, freed the captives, stood with the helpless, and were the voice for the voiceless.

Our parents taught us to know our rights, respect the rights of others, and obey the law of the land that we lived in. The most important thing they taught us is how to live the Christian life. I have witnessed the positive life of their journey, and I am rejoicing for the guidance that they gave us for the life to come.

I wanted to quote the answer that Mamma gave to Pastor Melkaamu Nagarii during the interview he had with her in March 2013. Her answer was so fulfilling and so deep, and I have decided to share that part.

Pastor Melkaamu Nagarii interviewed her for Sagalee Abdii from the Oromo Lutheran Church in Minnesota. What message does she has for those who are called to ministry and church? Her answer to his question was what Jesus said in **Romans 8: "Be faithful until death and I will give you the crown of life."**

To her, she said, "This statement is her stepping stone," and she tried to step on it throughout her life. Therefore, to her fellow Christians, in the same way, she said to live with hope, love, unity with Christ, to have the fear of God and to respect God. Also, let God give us the understanding of His Word by putting it in service. Not only being a listener of His Word but also showing it by action. In doing these things He will take us all to everlasting life.

At last P. Melkaamu asked her if she has the last word about the church. She said that as for her husband and her, the growth of the church is the benefit of their effort and that gave them strength and joy. They believed that all believers of Christ can lean on **Jude 1:24: "To him who is able to keep you from stumbling and to present you before his glorious presence without fault and with great joy."**

I am blessed that God gave me the opportunity to have my mother with me in her old age. My mother, being a person who multitasks and who taught her children handcrafting, cooking, and gardening at early age. I have been following her path, working and enjoying a lot of different handcrafts that she taught me. Thus, I gained a great deal of knowledge on how to do handcrafts, such as beading, crocheting, and knitting, because I had the desire for it.

I am also so proud of my mother that she was able to preserve her God-given knowledge and share it with my siblings and others who were willing to learn. She believes in perfection and does not rush in to doing her job. She has a good eye to pinpoint the faults on a design, and she has an eye for photography. If she sees a different design that she does not know, she captures the design in her mind and goes home and practices on that particular design until she gets it right. I knew that I had to check my work two or three times before I could show it to her.

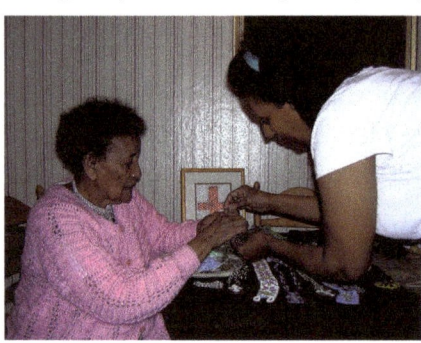

Mamma teaching Abby beading

This also made my big brother Samuel become a superb visual artist. My sister Tsion also gained more knowledge on design because she stayed behind when the rest of us left home. I appreciate my mother's persistence to lead me on the way to become a good designer. She even remembers the pattern of a sweater she made for Ayyaantu, her first-born baby daughter. She brought more than twenty-five types of old patterns that she had saved since 1940 for me to learn from.

At the end, I asked Mamma what else was left to write. She told me to write, "They have finished their race and they have kept their faith." I wrote this just as she told me, and it was clear that she was referring to the Bible verse in **2 Timothy 4:7: "I have fought the good fight, I have finished the race, I have kept the faith."**

It should be noted that what Mother narrated to me has been stored in her mind all her life. I am thankful to God for her for remembering the story as clear as yesterday at the age of ninety-seven years and being able to share it with all of us.

I thank my big brother Samuel Daffa for eyeballing and proofreading my script and all my siblings, and my sons Nathan, Boenna, Kebron, and the Reverend Dr. Dabelaa Birrii for encouraging and advising me to finish my work and making it possible for me to write this inspirational short story about our parents.

All glory and honor to our God.

ACKNOWLEDGMENTS

My gratitude to our Lord continues to grow each year that He has prepared and continues to prepare certain missionaries from across the sea, and sent them to my generation and the present generations in Oromia to bring the good news of the gospel to us and many places in the world.

I am thankful to Rev. Louis Harms of Germany (1808–1865), who had a dream of bringing the saving gospel of Jesus Christ to the Oromo people. God brought fulfillment to his dream in 1928 after many ups and downs of attempting to reach the Oromo people with the saving gospel since 1849. Had it not been for Rev. Louis Harms's dream, we wouldn't have become believers and followers of Our Lord Jesus Christ.

In the same breath, I am grateful to the American Presbyterian Mission who brought the gospel to Dambii Dolloo a few years before the arrival of the German Hermannsburg Mission in Aira and, which was instrumental in bringing Rev. Gidaadaa Solan to the Lord. Rev. Solan, in turn, was my mentor at an early age in Dambii Dolloo.

I thank God also for the life of Dietrich Wassmann and his family and the German Hermannsburg Mission, which successfully realized the dreams and vision of Louis Harms for the Oromo people and carried out his dreams starting on December 30, 1928, when the first group of missionaries arrived in Aira, Oromia, and started preaching and teaching the gospel. They stayed with us, spreading the Word of God and helping our people in so many different ways for almost a century.

I also would like to remember and thank those missionaries who lost their lives while on duty. May the merciful God bless them all.

I thank God for those missionaries who helped Onesimos Nasib be a messenger of God. I am thankful to God for leading Onesimos from slavery to freedom and, most of all, for giving him the ability, energy, and courage to translate the Holy Bible into Afaan Oromo, with the help of Aster Ganno (Gannoo Salbaan).

I am grateful for those first three Oromo pastors—Rev. Mamo Corqaa, Rev. Gidaadaa Solan, and Rev. Daffa Jammo—who picked up the Holy Bible to spread the message of salvation and continued the legacy of Onesimos Nasib. They guided and mentored me in my spiritual life in Dambii Dolloo.

Rev. Mamo Corqaa was ordained in 1939, and Rev. Gidaadaa was ordained in 1940 from the American Presbyterian Mission side. My husband, Rev. Daffa Jammo, was ordained in 1941 as the first Lutheran pastor from the German Hermannsburg Mission side in Aira, and later became the first Gimbii Awraja board (EECMY Western Synod) president.

They taught me the Word of God and prepared me so that I could also teach others. Those were our prominent spiritual leaders under God. They were the legends with the vision to carry the big torch of light, which is the Word of God, to the entire Wollaga Province in Ethiopia. And that light is still burning and will continue burning forevermore until the return of Jesus Christ. I think of those legends as a light in a dark tunnel during those dark days. May God be glorified for their services and lives.

Special thanks to the Aira faith community for supporting us in our work. We became one big family from the very beginning of our work and built the first Christian fellowship. Those were the following: Obbo Turaa Guutee and his wife, Adde Tujubee Ujukaa; Obbo Lamu Simaa and his wife, Adde Waandhibnnee Tirssuu; Obbo Ciibssaa Dangalaa and family; Obbo Gudataa Dastaa and family; Obbo Kachisaa Onchoo and family; Obbo Makonnen Abrahaam; Obbo Miijanaa Barite; Obbo Qannoo Saattaa; Obbo Qaanquree

Ciibassa and family; Obbo Gabraselassee; Obbo Yaddessaa Firdie; Obbo Naddo Bagoossa; and Obbo Woltaji Firdie.

We established a warm Christian community and lived as one happy family. All those families led good, solid Christian lives and will not be forgotten.

I am forever grateful for those who trusted us by listening to us and believed the Word of God when they were not even able to read and write at that early stage.

My deepest gratitude goes to my loving husband, Rev. Daffa Dajmmo, with whom I spent many memorable years of my life. He faithfully carried out the responsibilities God laid on him and did the work with honesty, being guided by God Himself.

A special thanks to our children, grandchildren, and extended families for standing by me always to this day, the last chapter of my life.

I praise God for giving me a long life to see the fruit of our labor that we left behind for the generation to come. I hear and see that those who became professionals in their careers were inspired by what God has done through us, the humble servants of the Lord.

All glory and honor to God.

1

GENERAL PORTRAIT OF OUR LIVES

It is hard to separate my life from that of my husband as I dictate this short reminiscence of my life to my daughter Abby Daffa.

I started teaching the Bible at the age of twelve under the guidance of Ms. Isabel Blair, my adopted mother. I can say that without the help of God, Ms. Blair, and my husband, I would not be who I am today. God is the One Who took me out of nowhere and brought me into His service.

This is purely a call of God, in my opinion. Obeying God's call and accepting His plan for our lives led to fulfillment of our Christian call.

Three things came to my mind when I decided to dictate the story of my life to my daughter. The first one was that I wanted to let our people know how we lived and led our community. Second, I wanted the young generation and others to know how we put into practice the Word of God in our lives as well as in the lives of those in our community. Third, since my husband was busy spreading the gospel I felt compelled to dictate this autobiography to our daughter, the teaching of the gospel was more important than telling about our own story.

The new generation has no clue of knowing how we reached the bright day of the Christian life they are observing today. We paid a big price every step of the way. When we both started our journey of the Christian life, we completely gave our lives to God Almighty. While we were paying attention to our family matters; we cuddled our community and our congregation.

If I were to narrate our entire life story, it could be three or four books. But I will try to summarize only the highlights of our story. Whatever we did in our lives was not for fame or praise for ourselves but to plant the seed of hope and faith in people's lives, with the hope that it can lead us all to eternal life.

Up to the last day of his life, my husband was talking about his congregations with dignity and joy in God. Also, he was concerned about the younger generation and was eager to know about how much they advanced in their education. He just wouldn't pass a day without asking about the younger generation, because they are the future of our people and our country. He truly enjoyed talking and telling old stories to the youngsters, and he loved to teach them poems. He told me that we are the memory of yesterday but the youngsters are the hope of tomorrow.

In life, I've found that whatever we planted yesterday is going to bear fruit tomorrow, so it was our desire to leave behind fruitful seedlings. My husband instilled wisdom within people by telling them a variety of the true stories of our church and life. He was a good listener and never ignored anyone. He treated everyone equally and paid attention to what was going on around them. He never rushed to give answers to anybody. He took his time and gave wise answers.

It is a joy to share the life we lived together and tell the true story of our Christian journey. We loved what we did and felt that it shaped our lives.

We clearly understood the teaching of Paul in **Galatians 6:2: "Carry each other's burdens, and in this way you fulfill the law of Christ."** We knew that God wanted us to live in harmony, to protect our marriage, and to be a good example for the coming generation. Part of that began with how we treated others with God's love and how we handled conflict in our own home. We tried to resolve our disagreements as quickly as we could by listening to each other and coming up with peaceful resolutions.

The Reminiscence of Our Lives In My Own Words

I have been questioned so many times if we ever had arguments or if we hashed each other out of disagreement. My answer was very clear and direct. I cannot deny that there were no ups and downs during the difficult and tiresome work we both endured. But we did not have time to argue and be angry at each other. God never failed us; He stood by us to bring fruitful services to our community that are still outshining for generations to come.

The goal of my husband's work was to let our Lord be pleased in every action that he took. The picture we both had on this journey was to have Him in our daily lives and continually pour our hearts out to Him without any hesitation. Every Christian who believes and has faith in Him will never draw attention to herself or to himself, and will never be ashamed but will show through the evidence of their lives that God is completely in control. That is where my husband drew a line for his life.

As human beings, we all have our moments. But when we gave our lives to Him and put our trust in Him with all our hearts and minds, He made the commitment to never leave us. He energizes us to complete the work we have been given to do for Him.

It is my earnest prayer and wish that this short story of ours will be enjoyed and shared to inspire those who are interested to know the beginning and growth of Evangelical Christianity in Wollaga and elsewhere.

It will be a source of education and blessing to share the journey of our lives with our Christian friends and relatives. All glory and honor to the Almighty God.

2
MY EARLY LIFE

Birth

My name is Kanatu Karorsa. I was born and raised in Dambii Dolloo, Wollaga on September 20, 1921, to my father, Karorsa, Babsa, Barii, Hambe, Boffo, Cawaaqee, Jijoo, Boruu, Kallachoo and my mother, Mijanee, Caqasee, Sibuu, Fufaa, Foggii.

Dambii Dolloo was named after my uncle's grandfather's burial place. Nagaoo Tulu Dolloo was married to my aunt Jibboo Caqasee, who was my mother's younger sister.

Dolloo was a well-known hunter, and people in that area considered him a hero. When he died, his "Gaachanaa and Faachaa" were placed on the *Dambii* tree, which was planted on his burial place. Gachanna is a shield made of hide, and Faachaa is the tail of the animal killed, and these are symbols of bravery. These memorialize the man who has killed wild dangerous animals, like lions, elephants, buffalos, tigers, etc., to prove to the people that he was brave and strong, and who never showed any signs of fear.

The hunter and his companions removed the hide and head of the animal and placed them in a certain place as a showcase for years, even after his death. That way, every sojourner passing by remembered the story of that brave man. The name of the brave man—Dolloo—and the Dambii tree planted on his grave became the name of the town: Dambii Dolloo.

This place became a resting station for merchants traveling from market to market to sell their goods. Women around that area prepared bread and a homemade beer (*farso*) to sell to the travelers. Those merchants were the ones who named that place Dambii Dolloo, and it became the most famous town in Wollaga Province.

Dambii Dolloo is located west of Qexoo River. Qexoo joins the Baroo River and flows through Gambella to the Sudan and merges with the Nile River in Sudan.

Siblings

Elizabeth, Kanatu and Fajii

I had one brother and one sister, Faajjii and Elizabeth Karorsa. Our parents passed away when I was about three years old. We were all raised by missionaries of the American Presbyterian Mission, who were serving as schoolteachers and nurses.

The American Presbyterian Mission arrived in Dembii Dolloo in 1919 (GC).

Ms. Isabel Blair adopted me as her child. My younger sister, Elizabeth, was raised by a nurse named Ms. Ruth Beatty. My brother was raised by Mr. Henry. These missionaries were our schoolteachers and medical specialists.

"When you were under the fig tree, I saw you" (John 1:48). God is always good, and He knew us when we were in our mother's womb. I thank God for preparing warm homes for the three of us after the death of our parents.

My brother Fajjii was tall and loved to gallop on horses. He was playful and also a joker. Everybody loved him and wanted to be around him. He did not like attending school. It was a real challenge to Mr. Henry to keep both Faajjii and his own son, Billy, in school.

When Fajii was born, our aunt Jibboo, my mother's younger sister, told us that Obbo Gammachiis Nasib, the son of Onesimos Nasib, moved to Dambii Dolloo to serve as translator for the missionaries and also to teach at the school. Eddosaa, Gammachiis's first son, was born in Dambii Dolloo. Eddosaa and Faajii were born around the same time. Our mothers became good friends and helped each other. They even fed each other's babies with their own breasts.

My mother, Mijanee, breastfed Eddosaa whenever Eddosaa's mother went to the market, and Eddosaa's mother did likewise whenever our mother went to the market or elsewhere. Our aunt told us that they loved each other and shared life together so much until our own mother passed away.

Our brother Faajjii and our cousin Tareessaa Dannoo were forced to go to the war when Italy invaded our country. Faajjii was married to Fayyisee Alabee before the war and left his bride with our uncle Danno Babssaa. Faajjii had three children: Berhanu, Ruth, and Dawit. They were all born after he came back from the battlefront.

My big brother travelled to Aira by horse to visit me and check on me every month during the Italian occupation of our country for five years.

A good friend of my brother by the name of Obbo Oliiqqaa Dingil had the most beautiful wife in Dambii Dolloo. At that time, one of the Amhara officials in Dambii Dolloo used his power, hoping that the Italian authorities could defend him, and took Obbo Oliiqqaa's wife for his own. Consequently, because of this injustice and abuse of power, Oliiqqaa killed that Amhara official, burned his house, and went into hiding. He fought bravely for

Fajii traveling from Dambii to Aira to visit me

five years, and the Italian soldiers were not able to capture him.

The Italians hired someone to follow him up, find his whereabouts, and put poison in his food. Sadly, they were successful in poisoning Oliiqaa, and he died.

That was the saddest day for my brother and our cousin Tarressa Daannoo. The Dambii Dolloo community supported Obbo Oliiqqaa until the last day of his life. My brother, our cousin, and friends were courageous enough to deliver to Obbo Oliiqaa all the materials that he needed to survive in the hiding place. My brother did this every time he came to visit me from Dambii Dolloo to Aira. My brother was known in our community as a community organizer and was respected and loved by many.

Elizabeth's engagement photo to Captain Tessemaa Erenaa.

My younger sister, Elizabeth Karoorssaa, was born on June 27, 1931 (GC), in Dambii Dolloo. When our parents passed away, she was a three-month-old baby, and Ms. Beatty, our nurse, adopted her.

Ms. Beatty recognized that she was a very intelligent little girl. She gave extra attention to her education. She closely watched her and guided her on the right path by teaching her not only the school curriculum but also the American culture. She was very smart. Just like me, she started teaching the Bible at the age of twelve and tutoring students to help the teachers and Rev. Gidaddaa Solan.

After completing her education offered in Dembii Dolloo, my sister moved to Finfinnee for further education and pursued her high school education. After completing high school, she served as a teacher and a clerk in the Commercial Bank of Ethiopia, in addition to serving the church as a leader. God created her with a variety of talents and huge purposes to use her in so many ways.

Then she met Captain Tessemaa Erenaa and married him in 1954 (GC), and they lived a joyful Christian life. Their wedding took place at the American Mission Girls School compound in Finfinnee, and was noted that the only Ethiopian Protestant wedding that has been held there, thus far.

Captain Tessemaa Erenaa was a high-standing officer in the Imperial Body Guard of the Ethiopian government. He served with the American troopers in Korea. He was a military man who was one of the finest soldiers of the era. He was respected and loved by many and became an icon for his people. He was direct and a charming man to all of us.

1954 wedding of Elizabeth Karorsa to Captain Tessemaa Erenaa

He studied law and worked as a lawyer for a cement factory for a long time after he came back from Jimma, Ethiopia, where he was detained for about four years for taking part in a military coup that attempted to overthrow Haile Silassie's government in 1960 (EC).

He continued working as a lawyer for the cement factory and the church. He also supported the Oromo community in every way possible. Both Elizabeth and Tessemaa were involved in church activities and helped us in raising our children. Their home was open to all who wanted to advance their education.

My sister Elizabeth will be remembered in the United States from her visit there in 1960–1961 on a study program. She spent one semester at Stroudsburg State Teachers' College in Pennsylvania, and then went on an observation of school teaching and administration in the central and southern part of the United States. In 1961, Elizabeth was a representative to the Purdue meeting for Presbyterian women and spoke to the six thousand people gathered there.

In 1958, she attended the joint meeting of All Africa Conference of Churches and the World Council of Churches that took place in

The Reminiscence of Our Lives
In My Own Words

Elizabeth preaching the Word of God

Ibadan, Nigeria, representing Ethiopia as the first woman. She again represented Ethiopia at the meeting of AACC and WCC in Northern Rhodesia in 1962. In 1965, she again attended the joint meeting of AACC and WCC held in Enugu, Nigeria.

She was the first woman to be elected to serve as a member of the church officers in the Ethiopian Evangelical Church Mekane Yesus in 1976. She also represented the Ethiopian Evangelical Church Mekane Yesus at the meeting of the Lutheran World Federation Seventh General Assembly in Dar es Salaam, Tanzania, in 1977 (GC).

One thing I know about my sister is that she never settled for less than the best. Anything she put her mind and her hands to, she did it remarkably well. She was an outstanding student from elementary throughout her university studies. She was bold, fearless, eager, and courageous to reach her goals. She was a fighter in all fronts.

In regard to unjust treatment of the people by the government, she stood for the oppressed. Once, she confronted Emperor Haile Silassie and his entourage on one of his escorted trips in Finfinnee to call his attention to the unjust treatment of Obbo Barro Tumsa and some of the members of the Mccaa-Tulamaa Self-Help Association detained by his government. She stood right in front of the emperor's car, and he stopped his car and asked her what the matter was. She told him about the case, and he let them go on a short notice.

With regard to the education of the young generation, she fought for them to achieve their goals and found scholar-

Last time Captain Tassamaa was with Elizabeth and Deribe in Minneapolis, MN, in 1992

ships for the needy. She also fought for the church and advocated on behalf of the faithful to worship their God in freedom.

My sister completed her education at Haile Selassie University and earned a diploma in education. She went to American University in Beirut, Lebanon, and earned her BA in education. As an educator, she had a strong desire to educate herself as well as others.

From 1960 to 1977, she was a teacher, and later, she became the director of American Mission Girls' School in Finfinnee. When Bethel merged with Mekane Yesus in 1974, she played an active role in the merger of the two.

As she was working as director of the school, she was elected as the first woman church officer in the Ethiopian Evangelical Church Mekane Yesus in 1976.

Her involvement in Qabale activities during the notorious Communist regime of Mangistu Hailemariam put her life in danger at the time of the so-called Red Terror, which forced her to flee to the USA in 1977, immediately after she attended the meeting of the Seventh General Assembly of the Lutheran World Federation in Dar es Salaam, Tanzania.

As soon as she arrived in the USA as a refugee, she enrolled in Wichita State University in Wichita, Kansas, where she got her master's degree in education.

While attending the university, she started looking for scholarships for needy students back home and managed to find in-country scholarships for sixteen students at once. All of them earned their degrees.

She was concerned about communities and loved to unite families and friends to work and grow together in a community. After she earned her master's degree, she worked for the United Presbyterian Church in Salina, Kansas, as a fraternal interpreter for the Presbytery of Northern Kansas and Midwestern USA during 1980 and 1981. From 1982 until the last day of her life, she lived in Minneapolis, Minnesota. She was very friendly and was always giving without looking for anything in return. She heralded at every occasion the values of honesty, integrity, and commitment for a genuine cause.

In her own unique way, she inspired everyone who crossed her path. She contributed a great deal of experience and wisdom in the processes of establishing Oromo Evangelical Churches in the USA in the cities of Minneapolis, Philadelphia, Canada, and Washington, DC.

I am thankful and so proud of my sister and her life that she shared with all our Oromo people, whom she loved. She also loved all humankind equally and worked for their well-being.

Deribe at age two with Elizabeth Karorsa

She did fight a good fight and kept her faith. **"I have finished the race, I have kept the faith. Now, there is in store for me the crown of righteousness, which the Lord, the righteous Judge, will award to me on that day and not only to me, but also to all who have longed for his appearing"** (2 Timothy 2:7–8).

God blessed her with all the noble qualities that one wishes to have. She loved her faith, God, and her fellow human beings.

My sister did not have a child of her own but helped us raise our children as her own. Deribe, our last child, was given to her as an adopted child. Deribe was four years old at that time. In the Oromo culture, the last baby should never leave the parents. But we loved my sister so much that we decided to let her have her to enjoy life with her.

I took Deribe at age 4 to Finfinee

My sister went to be with her loving God on February 9, 1997, in Dallas, Texas. Her husband, Tessema Erena, also died on April 20, 2005, in Finfinnee, Ethiopia.

Elizabeth's tombstone located in Minnesota.

Education

Ms. Blair put me in school and taught me handcrafts and general education given at that time.

My main study was the Bible, and she wanted me to learn fast and help her to teach the rest of the people. Besides the Bible, we learned science, math, and history. I was twelve years old when I started to help her teach the Bible.

Every Sunday late afternoon, she took us to the surrounding villages and arranged for us to take turns teaching the people. That was a big learning experience and an eye-opening time for me. Our teachers were Ms. Blair, Rev. Gidadaa Solan, Rev. Mamo Corqaa, and Obbo Ayyaanaa Algaa, Obbo Abbate Gebrselassie, Obbo Ayenew Addaal, and others.

My school life was really enjoyable. It helped me to realize that I had a bright future. I was focused on my education and was ready to take any opportunity. We were little children, and we enjoyed every moment of it.

One of my favorite times was every Friday night when Rev. Gidadaa Solan conducted Bible studies for the adults and my age group organized the bulletin for Sunday worship program. Right after school every Friday, we had to rush to the church, and half of us arranged the alphabets one by one and printed Sunday Scriptural readings for the congregation and placed them in the church. As soon as we finished that, Reverend Gidadaa read the Bible and gave us passages from the Scripture to memorize and recite on Sunday at worship service. The amazing thing was that those old people were smart enough to learn by heart and recite the Bible verses that Reverend Gidaadaa read to them.

Every Sunday night, girls were assigned to go around the neighborhood to help people to read the Bible. The neighbors took turns and hosted prayer fellowship at their homes. Some of those women were Harmee Nassie, Haadha Callaa, Adde Zeritu, and so many others. They applied the Bible to their hearts and minds.

My first church where I grew up

The way they taught the Bible is still sealed in my mind, and I cherish that memory each day of my life, and I praise my Lord Jesus Christ for giving me this life to tell this beautiful story of our people.

When the American missionaries started teaching us, Haile Selassie's government did not allow us to learn the English language as a subject at that time. This was because Dejazmach Jotte Tullu's son, Mardaasaa Jootee, was sent to a foreign country through Sudan, Khartoum, to get a modern education.

When he came back to Ethiopia after finishing his education, he was involved in activating the people to know their rights and speaking against injustices done to them. Haile Sellassie's government did not like that, and they put Mardaasaa's father, Dejazmach Jootee Tulluu, in prison and killed Mardaasaa and determined not to allow any Oromo student to take English classes.

At that time, the government ordered a man called Tefera Belehu to sit in our class to see to it that the English language was not taught to the Oromo students. Instead of English classes, all the male students had to take military training and the female student had to learn handcrafts. This was so painful for us to be separated from the rest of the students. The only students who were allowed to learn English were the Amhara and the Greek students.

I was good at math, and my teacher asked me to stand on a chair in front of the blackboard to help him teach and practice math problems for the rest of the students. Our school had a few classrooms, and one room was used for books and school supplies. The room served as a library. It was a wonderful campus, and we felt like we were so advanced compared to the rest of the provinces.

My dreams were shattered when Italy invaded our country. As soon as the Italian war started, all missionaries were ordered to leave Ethiopia for their own safety. The departure of the missionaries brought total darkness and an unexpected journey to all the students in Dambii Dolloo. As the Italians occupied the mission compound, those girls who had parents went back to their parents and the male students were forced to go to war.

My sister and I were left behind with only one nurse named Ms. Kline and one missionary named Phil West on the American mission compound. We were puzzled and did not know what to expect next.

Elizabeth among her educators and her cousin Degemtii Danoo.

My mother, Ms. Blair, and my sister's mother, Ms. Beatty, left with the rest of the missionaries. When they left, they made sure that we were well taken care of by the missionaries who were left behind for a short time. They left a note with Mr. Phil West that if it became difficult to keep us in Dambii Dolloo, we were to be taken to Finfinnee, where the rest of the American missionaries lived, and let Mr. Henry, who was in Finfinnee at that time, take care of us. Ms. Blair and Ms. Beatty hoped to return in a short time.

As for me, another journey was opened, and that was an arranged marriage. As soon as the American missionaries left, with the exception of Mr. Phil West, Pastor Wassmann arrived in Dambii Dolloo with the rest of the German missionaries from Aira who were on their way to leave the country. Pastor Wassmann remained behind to put things in order.

Marriage

German Hermannsburg missionaries were told to leave the country as well, and Pastor Wassmann came to Dambii Dolloo, moving the German missionaries to Khartoum, where a boat would take them to the nearest port to go to Germany. It was at this time that Pastor Wassmann saw me and took my picture without my knowledge to show it to Daffa Dajmmo, my husband-to-be, when he returned to Aira. He told him that he had found a Christian girl in Dambii Dolloo who was raised by an American missionary, and he proposed that he should marry me.

Reverend Wassmann knew that it was not a good idea to leave a single man behind, for he did not know how long it would take for the missionaries to return to Ethiopia. It was an arranged marriage, arranged by the German missionary on Daffa's side and the American missionary Phil West on my side.

Reverend Wassmann and Daffa sent a letter to Mr. Phil West to ask me if it was all right to make the wedding arrangements. Mr. West did not want to make the decision by himself, so he wrote a letter to my mother, Ms. Blair, who was in Khartoum at the time, and asked her if it was a good idea to wed me to Daffa.

Ms. Blair wrote back and said that if Kanatuu was willing to marry and if he was a Christian, then that would be fine. But if Kanatuu did not want to get married, she told Mr. Phil West, then they would take her to Finfinnee, where the rest of the American missionaries were still living.

In the meantime, Reverend Wassmann sent a mailman four times to see if Ms. Blair had replied to the request.

After he received the letter from Ms. Blair, Mr. West sent a letter to Reverend Wassmann, giving him the green light. Reverend Wassmann was so happy and proceeded with his plan and set the wedding date for January 12, 1936, and wrote a letter to Mr. West.

Mr. West agreed and prepared the feast for the wedding and waited for the arrival of the wedding party. The wedding took place nine months before the Italians occupied the American Mission compound in Dambii Dolloo.

Daffa arrived in Dambii Dolloo in January of 1936 (GC), with more than twelve people on a Sunday. When the wedding party arrived, we all were in the church, and Obbo Galataa, one of our school workers, knew where they came from and ran to them and greeted them. I was only fifteen years old. I did not even know where they came from and which one was Daffa at that time.

Addooyyee Aagee Bulie saw him walking with Ms. Kline, who was our school nurse, and took him for the hospital tour. She heard them talking in German and found out that he was the groom, Daffa. Then she ran fast back to us and told us that she found out who the groom was, and she said that he was a handsome and tall, skinny man. All of them were amazed to hear him speak in German, but they did not want me to marry him. They were concerned about the distance between Aira and Dembii Dolloo and that I would be far away from them. Soon after, they started planning how I could run away from him to Gore in Illubabor to live there. All my friends agreed and tried to persuade me to consent to their plan.

But I went to my bedroom and prayed and started thinking about my younger sister Elizabeth, who was only seven years old at the time. I told myself that if I ran away, the missionaries would be upset and may kick Elizabeth out and she would not have any place to go. I knew that my big brother Faajjii was capable to leave by himself with our relatives, but my little sister was the one whom I was worried about.

I said to myself, *There is no way that these missionaries will send me somewhere that can be harmful.*

After thinking about this for two long hours, I decided to go ahead with the plan to marry Daffa. My friends were disappointed and could not do much about it, but they supported me. They immediately started planning to escort me halfway to Aira, and they even started organizing what and how they could pack food for us to take, because we would be on a long journey as Aira was far from Dambi Dollo.

"By faith he went out, not knowing where he was going" (Hebrews 11:8).

The Reminiscence of Our Lives
In My Own Words

A big feast was prepared. All my relatives, church members, and the people from the villages were all invited. When the time came for me to depart from my family and friends, the sadness and crying started, and it was so hard for me to say good-bye, especially to my little sister Elizabeth. She did not know what marriage meant. She asked me if I could come back soon, and she even told me not to stay long but to come back within a week. That made me cry halfway to Aira. I was totally confused, and I did not think that I could stay in Aira without seeing my sister for a long time. The American missionaries promised my mother (Ms. Blair) that they would send a mailman every two weeks to Aira to check on me. Sure enough, they did until we had our three children and they too left Ethiopia.

Wedding day 1936, Rev. Daffa Jammo to Mrs. Kanatu Karorsa

Traveling from Dambii Dolloo to Aira was very challenging for me. I was so young and had never traveled by mule. It was a four-day journey. We had to rent a place to spend the night and travel during the day. My family packed food and water for us, which lasted for four days.

Near Aira, there was a place called Gabba Facasaa (Tuesday Market), where my husband's aunt lived. She was Jammo's sister and was married to a man called Korbeetti Raago. She waited for us with a wonderful feast, and we spent the night there.

Finally, we arrived at our destination, Aira. When we got to Aira, the German missionaries welcomed us with jubilation and prepared a big feast in our honor.

Rev. Fritz Bock conducted our wedding ceremony in Aira. Scripture reading for our wedding was from **Joshua 24:15: "As for me and my household, we will serve the Lord."** This was the first Lutheran wedding in Aira.

Rev. Daffa Jammo and I

My mother in law, Bajii Yoddo, did not like the service because she wanted it to be done according to traditional Oromo culture. They invited the people whom they knew from the Aira area, my husband's relatives and friends. It was a great joy.

Wedding day, 1936

After four days of celebration, another celebration was waiting for us at his mother's home at the place called Qaannao, where my husband was born and raised. The family was better off and they butchered oxen and celebrated with his family and friends from the Qaannao area such as Mando, Masnaoo, Gaallao, Suntaallao, etc. The celebration lasted for three days, and finally, we went back to Aira to start life.

Daffa, Mijana, and Maganee Jammo

My husband had three brothers: Ofga'aa, Mijanaa, and Bidduu. Also had two sisters: Kashee and Maganee, Maganee and Mijanaa were twins. Bidduu and Kashee passed away of short time sickness at their early age. The firstborn of the family, Ofga'aa Jammo, had five children: Margaa, Kitlee, Kassahun, Shashitu, and Nigatu. Ofga'aa Jammo died of short-time sickness. That was a very sad time for the family.

Young family 1940

Mijanaa Jammo had seven children: Margee, Maartaa, Emmanu'el, Efreem, Ebbisee, Gannatee, and Faanosee. Maganee Jammo had five children: Kummarraa, Simbaatu, Taddesse, Bafitu, and Shiferaw.

My husband and his brothers were very close and kept their eyes on each other. Their mother, Bajjii, was overprotective of her children, and their respect and love for their mother was enormous.

The Reminiscence of Our Lives
In My Own Words

When I came from Dambii Dolloo, I found out that my husband was a translator for the German missionaries. He traveled with them and translated from German to Afaan Oromo whenever they preached the gospel, and he also helped doctors and nurses in the clinic. It was hard for him to be at so many places with them to do this job, but he wanted to learn their language and teach them our language (Afaan Oromo) so that it could be easier in the future to work together. At the same time, he learned how to treat the sick people and the types of diseases and what types of medication to use for the variety of sickness.

My husband's brother Miijanaa taught him the alphabet and how to read and write at a very young age. At one point, my husband wanted to run away from his mother, Bajii, to Gimbii, where his brother went to school. But his mother favored him because he was the last child. She caught him planning to go to Gimbii with his brother, and she watched him very closely so that he could not escape from her.

He was too close to his mother and consulted her before he took any step to please her. But he knew very well that she would not let him go out of her sight. He decided to plan behind her back with his big brother Mijana to leave her and go to school.

My husband wanted to go to school with his brother so that he could be a judge to correct the judicial system. My husband told his mother that he did not like to see poor people being mistreated. One of his plans in life was to help poor people by becoming a judge to let their voices be heard.

He was a handyman before he became a pastor. He was a carpenter and was fond of making baskets (gaagura) to serve as beehives. He had beehives mounted on trees in a nearby forest or on trees in the backyard.

At that time, every single house had beehives, drank homemade honey wine (Dadhii), and made their coffee with honey. Coffee with honey was very tasty, and the villagers invited each other over and enjoyed drinking together.

His parents owned cattle, sheep, and goats. He was a shepherd as a child and had lots of nicknames, as his mother told me. He was favored not only because he was the last child but also because he was a joy to his community. He went around at very young age and helped his community as much as he could. Maybe the leadership trait was planted in him at that very young age.

Reverend Wassmann taught my husband German, and my husband taught him Afaan Oromo. They helped each other in spreading the gospel, planting churches, and leading the Christian life. In his youth, my husband captured the idea of the gospel very quickly. My husband was a good listener and a very intelligent young man who never rushed to answer. He thought twice or thrice before he shared his judgment on any issues. Once he made a decision, he executed it immediately and very well.

The two leaders: Rev. Daffa Jammo, the first Lutheran pastor in Ethiopia, and Rev. Dietrich Wassmann, the first German missionary in Aira Wollaga.

That was what captured Reverend Wassmann's mind about my husband. He said that Daffa's mind was like a sponge: once he got an idea, he wouldn't let it go, he kept it in his heart and mind.

When the time came for the missionaries to leave, my husband and Reverend Wassmann had already translated Luther's Catechisms, the Lord's Prayer, Order of Holy Communion, the Apostles' Creed, Divine Service Setting, and songs into Afaan Oromo.

The first song my husband translated was *Dafaatii gara Yesuus kottaa*, and after that, he translated so many more songs. He was ready to start his duty that the God Almighty had given him, and he truly had a desire to follow Jesus Christ with all his heart and mind.

Reverend Wassmann left Aira six months after my arrival. The only missionaries left behind with us were Reverend Horombostel and Rev. Fritz Bock. Life became gloomy, but I did not have much choice but to accept the reality.

The Reminiscence of Our Lives
In My Own Words

Reverend Wassmann ordained my husband into the ministry of Lord and Sacraments in April 1941 just before he left. My husband became the first Oromo Lutheran pastor to be ordained in Wollaga.

When I arrived in Aira, my husband explained to me how the missionaries built the clinic, school, and church in the Aira area. Reverend Wassmann's first son, Dietrich Wassmann (Dii Dii), was born in a tent. Soon after Dietrich was born, they built a small clinic so that Martha, the sister of Reverend Wassmann, could treat the sick there. There were only three people who were communicants, including my husband. When I joined, we became four. Those three communicants were Reverend Horombostel, Rev. Frtz Bock, and my husband. I was already a communicant before I came to Aira.

One week after our wedding, a respectful man by the name of Obbo Barkeessaa Ujukaa gave me his nine-year-old daughter Zewditu Barkeessaa. He told me to teach her all that I had learned in school and the Bible. I took her as my little sister and loved her so much. She was a very bright little girl and was open to learn any new things coming her way.

She grew up with us and got married to Obbo Olumaa Gaantii and gave birth to twelve children. She helped build a big church at a place called Buuyee. I thank the Lord for her ability and dedication to serve the Lord.

3

LIFE TOGETHER

During the early days of our marriage, we lived in Rev. Fritz Bock's house in the German Mission compound.

The house had four rooms. Our first two children were born there. We continued to have Bible studies and worship service in the big house Reverend Wassmann built. When the missionaries were ordered to leave because of the war, they closed that big house and gave the key to my husband and told him to keep the key because they would be back in a short time.

We continued having our services on the porch of Reverend Wassmann's house. My husband kept inviting a lot of people from our area, and we started growing in numbers until that porch was not big enough to hold all of us.

That was the first eye-opening energy that my husband gained. **"For where two or three come together in my name, there I am with them" (Mathew 18:20).** My husband decided to move us out from Rev. Fritz Bock's house to the school next door. The house had four rooms, and he reconstructed the room and changed it to one big church. We became a big congregation and continued having our church services.

At this time, I could tell that my husband felt alone in carrying all the responsibilities of looking after the German Mission compound and the people in the community around him. All of them were beginners in their Christian lives and looking up to him. He felt so burdened, and he decided to move fast on teaching and guiding them every way possible.

"Go into the world and preach the good news to all creation" (Mark 16:15). We immediately formed a small Bible study group, and my husband told me to Start teaching Alphabet. By teaching the alphabet, it would help the people to learn how to read and write and be able to read and understand the Bible. People at that time were very eager to learn and do whatever it took to live a better life. This encouraged and gave me the energy to teach them more.

Congregation worshiping under Wassmann's home

We split our tasks between the two of us to make things easier. My husband built the churches and taught the gospel. I taught reading, writing, songs, scriptures, handcrafts, and gardening—fruits, vegetables, and a variety of grains and flowers. We started receiving so many guests, mostly students, and life was so difficult because bandits (outlaws) roamed around at will while the country was at war with no law and order.

The Italian war changed our lifestyle and totally destroyed our country. Much destruction occurred, but nothing shook our faith. We were so eager and worked hard to spread the Word of God. We were concerned about our community. We wanted to plant in the hearts of every believer the godly life.

During the Italian occupation, the German Mission compound was under my husband's supervision, and we had difficult times to go through those days because there was much looting going on around us. We protected and preserved the compound by building thorny fences, laying bushes and rocks, and digging trenches or ditches around the compound.

"He Himself has said, I will never leave you nor forsake you" (Hebrews 13:5).

Wassman teaching songs

The guards were placed at a certain distance two by two in the ditches and were given one gun and a strong spear for each group. They slept during the day and watched the compound during the night.

My husband used the two cans and string technique for communication during the night. He collected empty soup cans and made a hole at the bottom of each can and connected them together to communicate and pass information to one another during the night with neighbors. It connected our house to that of Obbo Turaa Gutee, Obbo Lamu Simaa, and a few close neighbors. We informed one another if we heard any shootings or disturbances. They used this technique as a telephone line to communicate, and nobody noticed it except for a few of our friends.

My husband sent rumors to the bandits that they would be killed if they tried to attack the Mission compound. Whatever happened, my husband had no fear about anything. He was so determined and dedicated to face any circumstances coming his way, for he had great faith in and the support of the Almighty God.

When it seemed that there was no one around to help us, he said to me, "The Lord is our helper, and He has promised us not to let us down and leave us in any difficulty." He never showed any kind of fear because he truly believed in God.

Fortunately, my husband had learned basic medical treatment from German caregivers; therefore, he was able to give first aid to those who were wounded by the bandits. People from our area and even from far distances came to him for dental and a variety of sickness to get treatment. He went to Yuubdo and Gimbii to treat the sick. He did all this because of his commitment to God Almighty. Those Italians who lived in Yuubdo and Gimbii respected and admired his work.

As a result of that, my husband treated so many people's broken legs, shoulders, and stomach wounds by patching them together and giving them medication. I remember that Obbo Jobbir Dentaa Luba Kumarraa Jobbir's father from Aira, Obbo Tasisaa Daano from Kobaraa near Bodjii Dirmajii, Obbo Abdissa Tesso from Kobaraa, and Likassa Abba Chaffee from Warra Qaaluu were some of them.

The bandits (outlaws) in our area sent word to my husband that they would get him for helping and healing those people whom they had attacked and wounded. My husband sent a messenger back, saying, "All is well, and nothing can stop me from treating the sick coming from all directions." He told me that since God allowed and gave him the knowledge to do his job, he must fulfill His will.

As Christians, we are not here for our own purposes at all but for His purposes. We must maintain our daily commitment with the help of God. These were his statements for those people who were out there to destroy our community.

There was a time when we lost about seventeen people from the Aira area alone to malaria in two weeks. Very few in our community made it through that epidemic. My husband was the only one who was treating all those people and people from other communities. They brought the patients to Aira from far and wide or called him if the sick person could not make it to Aira for treatment.

It was very hard for him to do so, but by the grace of God, he never got sick or weakened. My husband and Adde Dastaa Bagoosaa were going all over the place to give vaccinations and medication to the sick. People avoided each other as much as possible during the malaria epidemic, because it was very contagious and dangerous. Both of us and Adde Dastaa never got sick because God used us to help so many sick people recover. God carried us through all those difficult times without a hitch.

I was the only one who made soup and porridge (Marqaa) and delivered to Adde Dastaa Bagoosaa, who was working in the clinic. She and my husband fed the sick all those times. It was only the three of us who gave service to all those people. Obbo Dheeressaa Batoo helped us for a short time. He also had malaria and was on the verge of death, but God spared his life.

Some of those people with malaria lost their minds and ran out of their houses. My husband would run after them and tie them down on their beds for treatment.

It was a very tough time that we went through, and we were blessed to see the outcome of our work by the grace of the Lord.

The Italians insisted that my husband move to Yuubdoo to treat malaria patients, but he refused to leave the Aira Mission compound because he was the only one who was able to treat the sick in Aira. My husband referred the Italians to Obbo Eranaa Waayyuu from Boodjjii, my husband's best friend, who was also well trained by Sister Martha Wasmann as a caregiver. As soon as they got this message, they contacted him and had him moved to Yuubdoo to treat the sick people there.

After a while, the malaria became so difficult to control that my husband requested the Italians to send Obbo Eranaa back to Aira for help. Obbo Eranaa came back to Aira and helped my husband for one week and went back to Yuubdoo to continue his work with the Italians.

Having been the first pastor in the Lutheran Church in Wollaga, my husband was a religious leader, a pastor, a teacher, a caregiver, and a community leader in the midst of opposition both from the bandits and the Orthodox clergy. The bandits disturbed the peace of the community. The Orthodox Church clergy opposed the Mission work. My husband preached the gospel of Jesus Christ boldly and carried out the Great Commission of our Lord (Matthew 28:19–20) without any fear.

The missionaries did not only preach the gospel but also contributed to the well-being of the community by establishing educational and health institutions, such as schools, hospitals, and clinics. My husband spread the message of the gospel in many places in Wollaga by travelling on foot and mule, as I have mentioned earlier.

My husband had a divine purpose for being on this earth, and the purpose of his vision and mission was to spread the Word of God that was rooted in him at his early age. He was a type of person who lived what he preached. I can honestly say he walked the talk. His work was inspiring and uplifting to the people around him.

He told me that he was going to do whatever it took to educate his people and build the church, clinics and hospitals.

"Until my people come to the knowledge of Jesus Christ as Savior and Lord and become educated, there is no rest for me," he said.

He told me that I had to be strong and support him, and that he did not want me to show him any despair or weakness whatsoever. He expected a lot from me.

Out of despair, frustration, and hardship, I decided to go back to Dembii Dolloo during the early stage of our lives together, but I did not know the road and did not know how to get there. I tried two or three times to flee early in the mornings while he was away for work. I attempted to hide behind the trees near the road to Dembii Dolloo in the hopes of finding merchants traveling to Dembii Dolloo.

Had I been fortunate to find those who were going to Dembii Dollo, I could have gone back to Dembii Dolloo with them. But it never worked for me the way I wanted, because I could not find anyone going to Dembii Dollo, and I had to return home in the evening.

On one occasion, my little sister Elizabeth and my big brother Faajjii came to visit me from Dembii Dolloo, and I told my little sister that I would run away to Dembii Dolloo and that she should come back with my brother and meet me in Dembii Dolloo. I left my little sister at home as my big brother went to the market, but I was unsuccessful finding those merchants again.

Finally, I accepted the reality and dropped the idea of running away and continued living with my husband. God had a plan for me, but I did not understand that plan fast enough, for I was too young at that time.

Everyone has been created for a purpose with the ability to reach out beyond her or his own grasp. It was God Who drew me to Himself, and my relationship with Him was an inner, personal one, not an intellectual one. My relationship with God was a miracle performed by God Himself, and His urge moved me to submit to His will and follow Him.

The love and fear of God kept me going forward. In hindsight, as I reflect back now, my husband was a true man of God who listened to the voice of God. He did what God wanted him to do, and he lived according to the desire of the Almighty God. I always think of my husband as an ambassador of God.

After our wedding, we started organizing our lives together. In 1939, another chapter of our life began as soon as our first daughter, Ayyaantu, was born. We started experiencing a new life.

The community was so happy and made porridge with gravy (marqaa with saammitaa), according to our Oromo culture. My mother-in-law was not very happy that the firstborn was a girl. In Oromo culture, they are more jubilant if the firstborn happens to be a boy.

Ayyaantu's tomb is located in the German Mission compound in Aira Wollaga.

Two years later, our second child, Saamu'el, was born, and my mother-in-law was so happy that she prepared a feast, and the celebration was more magnificent than the first one.

Our first-born child, Ayyaantu, became sick and died at the age of a year and eight months. That was a sad experience for both of us. She had the first Christian baptism service and burial in the history of the Evangelical Church in Aira.

As we continued our work and family life together, my husband's life became so busy. He was on the road more than he was with his family. I felt like it was my obligation to take most of the responsibilities around Aira Church and managing the community and my family.

"If you love me, keep My Commandments" (John 14:15). Our Lord never insists on our obedience. He stresses very definitely what we ought to do, but He never forces us to do it. We obediently make up our minds to have a relationship with Him. This was the step that we both promised to take when we became His servants.

The news of our evangelistic work spread like wildfire. Obbo Ashanaa Naggaade, who later became Luba Ashanaa Naggaade from

Teggie, heard about the teaching of the missionaries and came to Aira. He did not agree with the government-favored Orthodox Church religious teachings in Teggie. His disagreement became such a big issue for the government that they wanted to arrest him.

He went to Caliyaa Ekkaa, where Balambaras Gammadaa Urgessaa was a chief ruler. Blamambaras was a loyal supporter of my husband's work and the Evangelical Church; therefore, he advised him to run away to Aira, where we were. We hid him in our house for three months and taught him how to read and write the alphabet and to read the Bible for himself.

I am so thankful for Obbo Makonnen Abrahaam and Obbo Lamu Simaa, who helped me teach him, because I was very busy feeding the rest of the people. It would have been so hard on me to handle the situation by myself since my husband was traveling a lot.

Balambaras Gammadaa worked so hard to solve the problem encountered with the Orthodox Church so that Obbo Ashanaa could go back to Teggie and teach. In the meantime, my husband took time to teach him the Ten Commandments, the Lord's Prayer, the Creeds, and how to preach the gospel.

After three months, Obbo Ashanaa had enough knowledge to start helping my husband. He made him practice his teaching and tested how he presented himself in public. As soon as he was capable of teaching and preaching, he started traveling with my husband and they took turns preaching.

After a long time of observation and training in the newly started Bible school in Boodjjii, Obbo Ashanaa was ordained and became a pastor to serve the churches in the Aira and Teggie areas.

4

LOOKING FOR PEOPLE WHO WERE WILLING TO LEARN

My husband told me that he was going to look for some more people who were willing to take Bible lessons in Aira.

"Come follow me," Jesus said, **"I will make you fishers of men"** (Mathew 4:19).

He left for a month and came back with fifteen people. He left them with me so that I could teach them the alphabet with Obbo Makonnen Abrahaam.

Makonnen and I started sort of a literacy campaign, so to speak, in that region for the first time and taught the first batch of fifteen people. We taught them the alphabets, religious hymns, and Scriptural verses so that they could be familiar with the Bible.

My husband left the people to us and was away for three months to build churches. When he came back, he was so happy to see the people read and write and study the Bible more deeply.

He took over and taught them the Bible further for a long time until they were able to grasp the glimpse of true life of Christ. He took them back to where they came from and guided them to teach turn by turn as he watched them.

After a year of teaching and training, he taught them about the Last Supper. He wanted them to get a deeper understanding of the covenant between God and us as Christians that is exemplified by the

Lord's Supper. He kept on warning them that if they were not ready to take it, then it was all right to wait until they were ready to do so. It is sin by itself to take the Communion without understanding the importance of it.

He gave them time to think about it and to let him know when they were ready to take it. After they told him that they were ready, he taught them the Ten Commandments, the Creeds, and all they needed to know, and they all took the Communion.

The main goal of his teaching was to let them clearly mark in their hearts to impact their daily Christian life step by step. Those steps were reading the Word of God, meditating on it with understanding, praying, praising, thanking, confessing their sins and repenting, and glorifying God. These steps were the core guidelines of his teachings. He believed that if those fifteen men couldn't understand the depth of these steps, it would be hard for them to teach others when they go out to teach God's words to the world.

Those people went back to their places and taught their children and the people in their communities what they had learned and spread the Word of God all over that region like a wildfire. From that time on, tens of thousands of people in that region educated themselves from basic to higher learning making the gospel the center of their understanding and life.

During that period of time, Luba Taasisaa Dureessaa, Obbo Dheeressaa Batoo, Obbo Abdiisaa Baacaa, Obbo Galatee Dangalaa, Obbo Ciibssaa Dangalaa, Obbo Turaa Guutee, Obbo Lamu Simaa, Obbo Miijanaa Barrite, Obbo Kaachisaa Oncho, and Obbo Makonnen Abrahaam were living with us, and I am so grateful that they gave their time and energy to give us help in every way possible. Even though Luba Taasisaa Dureessaa was much younger than my husband, they advised and helped each other so much. We loved Luba Taasisaa so much, and we considered him as our son. We were close friends with his mother, Naasisee Sardaa, and we became a family.

When I came to Aira, I was young and did not know the facts of life very well. Adde Naasisee Sardaa, Tujubee Ujukaa, and Dastaa

Bagoosaa gave me advice on how to adjust to life in the new community that I had joined.

In Dambii Dolloo, all I knew was the American way of life because I was raised by an American from my early childhood and I was not introduced to community life. Specifically, I had no idea how to work on a farm at all.

One day, they invited me to help them in a farm field by joining them (daboo, helping one another in turn in a group) to pull out weeds (aramaa aramu) in the *xaafii* field. I accidentally pulled out the xaafii and grass together. Adde Tujubee Ujukaa and Adde Dasta Bagoosaa stopped me and taught me how to do it right.

Most of the time, I got help from my neighbors: Adde Tujubee Ujukaa, Adde Nuuree, Adde Ganamee, Haadha Shiferaw, and Adde Dastaa Bagoosaa. They were so helpful to me in teaching me the right way to work on the farm. I was a fast learner, and I started farming in my own field. It was at that time that I developed the knowledge of growing anything that I wanted on our farm.

I realized that I was introduced to the new community and eager to learn anything comes on my way; thus, I was fascinated to learn the way they celebrate their harvest time festival. This is a special time that they thank the Lord, similar to how Americans celebrate Thanksgiving Day.

In Qaanna'o, we celebrate a little different than the rest of the country. This is ritual for the Oromo culture. When the rainy season is over and a bright sunny season appears, the community comes together and prepares nine different foods in order to thank the Lord for giving them food, water, air, rain, and sun for their lives.

The food they prepared is bread, greens, chuukoo, meat or beans, daadhii made of haney, farssoo (bear), hanchootee, boonaaqallaa, baaduu, and whatever they harvest from their God-given land. This was how they celebrated their Thanksgiving. Nobody eats the first thing they harvest from their farm without inviting their neighbors or communities to gather and thank the Lord. I did not know though why they prepared only nine types of food or dishes. This is noted among the Oromo people.

Before eating, the following prayer should be said by those communities. This prayer would be started by the owner of the house or by the eldest person among the community: "God, who stands still and gives us something to eat and drink and protected our children, our country, our cattle and watched over us, let our lives be in your hands throughout our lives."

(In Afaan Oromo; Waqaa Hunduma Uumtee, Waqaa dhissa malee diriituu, Waqaa wan nyaanuuf dhugnuu nukeene; atii nuueegii, jiiregni kenyaa harkakerr nuf hataauu, ijoolee keenyarati nubulchii, galgalaa kenyaa nutolchi).

This was their main prayer. At that time, to celebrate this festival day, people did not go to the lakes; instead, they invited all the neighbors and their communities to celebrate this special day under the shade of a big tree and dance after they finished eating.

Luba Ashanaa Nagaadee sent his wife, Adde Worknesh, from Teggie to help me with the guests for one month. I thanked them both for their services and energy that they shared with us. All these men and women were in our Bible study circle and were supporters of my husband.

In those days, people were very dedicated and believed the Word of God and accepted Him as their own Savior and followed Him. Most of the people did not have any kind of formal education but accepted the Word of God by faith and became faithful Christians, only by hearing the Word of God from me and my husband and others.

"The people living in darkness have seen a great light; on those living in the land of the shadow of death a light has dawned" (Mathew 4:16).

What has amazed me all my life is that those people memorized the songs and the scriptures by heart so fast, specifically the Western religious songs with all their harmony. We did not have any problem teaching them because I already learned how to teach well while I was in Dambii Dolloo. I also taught others to teach.

Thanks to God Almighty for letting Pastor Wassmann teach my husband how to teach others very well, indeed. He and my husband translated the German religious songs to Affaan Oromo.

We served our community from the depths of our hearts. That service kept our relationship with God intact to glorify Him, reflecting God's character in our lives. The Son of God revealed Himself through us, and because of our commitment to Him, our service became our everyday way of life.

5

WHAT WE NEEDED FOR OUR DAILY LIFE

Light

Since there was no electricity at that time, we made our own candles:

(1) We twisted a bunch of cotton thread together and dipped it into melted honey wax and used it as a candle when it dries. We called it *dungoo*.
(2) We crushed castor beans, got rid of the outer cover, lined up the seeds, thrust them one by one on thin sticks, and used it as a candle.
(3) Candle made of cow suet (*mooraa*). We rolled suet (*mooraa*) around a thin stick, roped it around with cloth, and used it as a candle.

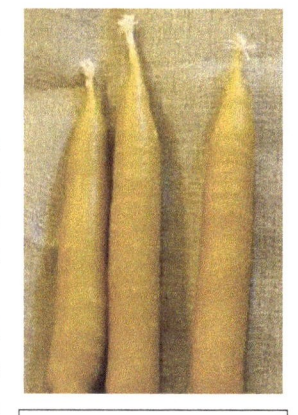

Making candles by hand

We had to light the candles all night long to ward off the bandits; otherwise, they would break into the houses and rob from the people in our community.

Cooking Oil

Generally, we used butter for cooking. In addition to that, we used oil made of *nuugii* (sunflower oil seed). We had to pound the oil seed by pestle in a wooden mortar and make cooking oil out of it. Sometimes we bought and used imported oil from Khartoum or Kurmuk brought to our market.

Grain

The common grains we used were corn, barley, wheat, sorghum, xeef, etc. We either produced them ourselves or bought them and stored them for use. I ground grains with my own hands on the stone especially selected and made for grinding all sorts of grain.

Pounding the grain and oil seed

I was relieved to some extent when the grinding mill was introduced. I drew water from the river in a clay jar (okkotee) and carried it home on my back. I also collected firewood to cook food to feed many people, including many guests. I would receive help from neighbors occasionally; otherwise, it was my sole responsibility to do that.

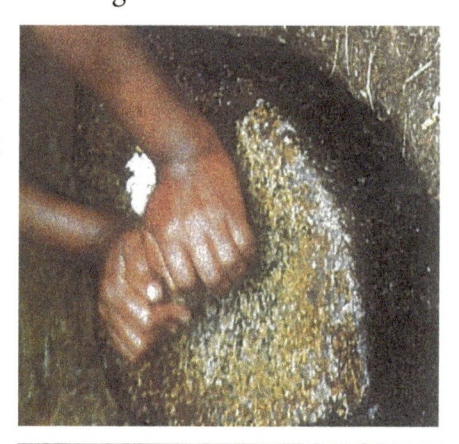

Grinding the grain

Firewood

We collected firewood from the field in the area or went to the nearest forest and carried it home on our backs. We stored the firewood in a special place where it was kept dry. We also chopped logs to get smaller pieces of firewood.

We used the firewood to cook food. Once we were done with our cooking, we did not let the fire die out completely because we did not have matches to make a new fire the next day. In order to have fire the next morning, we had to preserve it by putting the glowing coal (red hot) under the ashes and completely covering it with a pile of ashes. The next morning, we easily pulled out the still-glowing coal from under the ashes and started the fire again to cook. This had to be done every single day after we were done with our cooking for the day.

Carrying wood on my back

Water

We drew water from the nearest river in a clay jar (okotee) and carried it on our backs.

I will never forget one particular day when I went to the river twelve times to draw water in one day. My back was falling apart, but I could not complain or show a sign of fatigue because there were guests in our house. We used the water not only for drinking and cooking but also for washing clothes and washing our guests' feet, etc.

These duties were mostly some of our heaviest and most difficult daily routines in those days.

Carrying water on my back

After I finished feeding the family and our guests every night, there was always a Bible study and singing. I knit sweaters, crocheted or sewed clothes for my children whenever I had spare time in the evenings. We entertained seven to fifteen people in our home every day or night.

After I put everybody to bed, I went back to the kitchen and prepared dough for the morning breakfast so that it would be easy for me to start my morning. I mostly got four or five hours of sleep a night. At times, I felt very dizzy and exhausted, yet I worked without any break. All I knew was hard work, and I did not have time to complain and look for any excuses because I could not change anything.

I clearly understood that the realization of God's call was what gave me energy, joy, and determination to continually remember God's vision for us. That was where my energy came from, and I am so thankful to my Lord to keep me under His wings.

Whenever I got a chance, I ran to my garden and planted vegetables, fruits, and flowers. I taught our guests how to take care of the garden and gave them the seedlings (chiginy) to take home and plant them for their future needs. For those who lived near us, I took the seedlings to their homes and helped them plant and taught them how to take care of the garden.

I made sure that all those people knew what I knew and gave them what I had. At the end of the day, when I saw the progress of those people, it made me so happy.

Dietrich (Dii Dii) Wassmann, the son of Reverend Wassmann, was very young those days, yet when he saw the difficult domestic burden I was carrying, he started helping me by chopping logs for firewood. Martha, his sister, helped me make bread (budenaa), and Maria helped me make stew (ittoo). They tried their best to help me at their young age, and they learned how to cook our food very well.

6

"COME OVER AND HELP US": NADJJOO, BOODJII, MANDII, AND NAQAMTEE

Because Germany and Italy were allies, the Italians allowed the German missionaries to return to Aira after two years of absence to continue the work they had started earlier. Pastor Wassmann, with his group, came back and continued the work.

The work at Nadjjoo, Boodjjii, Mandii, and Naqamtee was started by the Swedish Evangelical Mission before the Italian invasion. The Swedish missionaries left when Italy invaded Ethiopia.

Adde Naasisee Liiban from Nadjjoo contacted and invited Pastor Wassmann to come to Nadjjoo and help them in their desperate need. In the letter she wrote, she said, "We became the lost sheep without a shepherd," noting that they were left without any spiritual nurture and guidance.

As soon as they received that letter, Pastor Wassmann and my husband took off to Naadjjoo to teach, preach, and strengthen the believers there. Both of them promised Adde Naassisee that they would do whatever it took to serve them until the Swedish missionaries returned.

Adde Naassisee came to Aira for medical treatment through Caliyaa Ekkaa, and visited Balanbaras Gammdaa Urgeessaa and asked him for assistance. Balambaras agreed and brought her to Aira.

Adde Naassisee's plan became so successful that my husband started serving Nadjjoo, Bodjjii, Mandii, and Naqamtee as well.

Pastor Wassmann was in the process of leaving the country again after the defeat of Italy. He had given him the necessary pastoral training and was confident that my husband was able to carry the responsibility of pastoral office.

After he was ordained, the responsibility of baptizing, giving the Lord's Supper, conducting burial services, officiating on wedding services, and all pastoral leadership was given to him. My husband became the first Oromo Lutheran pastor in Aira, Wollaga, when he was ordained in 1941.

Before he ordained my husband, Wassmann asked me if I would accept the responsibility with my husband and if it was all right with me for him to be ordained. I told him that if this was what God wanted him to do and he accepted the call, who was I to say no to God's call?

Wassmann was so delighted in my answer that he gave me a hug and thanked me for accepting the call of our Lord. My husband's life reminded me of a verse in **Isaiah 6:8: "I heard the voice of the Lord, saying: 'Whom shall I send? And who will go for us?' Then I said, 'Here am I! Send me!'"**

Daffa was truly ready to be sent wherever God wanted him to go and carry His cross and walk with Him. He told me once, "The call of God is not just for a select few but for everyone. I accept that call, and I will do whatever it takes."

The mission gave my husband the full responsibility of the church, clinic, and school. My husband was the first Lutheran pastor of Mekane Yesus in Ethiopia. The only other pastor was Qes Badema, an Orthodox priest ordained in the Orthodox Church. Qes Badema accepted the Lutheran doctrine, and kept his pastoral title to serve the Lutheran Church Mekane Yesus in Addis Ababa through the Swedish missionaries at that time.

This was how they crossed the river.

The Italians authorities ordered the German missionaries to leave the country again two years after they came back. British soldiers were coming to take over the country as Italy and Germany were together in fighting against the British in World War II.

The German missionaries quickly left the country, leaving my husband alone by himself with the responsibility to carry on the work in all the areas of Aira, Nadjjoo, Bodjjii, Mandii, and Naqamtee. **"As for me, being on the way, the Lord led me" (Genesis 24:27).**

When he was traveling around to all these places, so many lives suffered for the cause. We lost our three mules because of exhaustion right in front of our house. After a long trip, as soon as my husband returned, the mules simply fell down and died. It felt like we were losing a human life, and I cried for them. These animals couldn't speak up and say they were tired.

One of our mules knew and could sense whenever my husband became very tired, and she would find a tree with shade to lean on for him to take a nap near the road. When they came home, the people who carried my husband's briefcase and traveled with him told us the story of the mule and how tired my husband became when traveling.

7

INCIDENTS ON TRIPS

When he came back from wherever he had preached, he gave a report to elders of the Aira Church. One time, he told us that when he first went to Mandii to preach, he went to the house of an elderly man, Obbo Eranaa Sardaa.

My husband said, "As soon as I entered his house, he told me to get closer to him. He bowed down his head and poured oil on his head and asked me to bless him, thinking of me as one of the disciples."

He continued and said that Obbo Eranaa told him that it was the happiest day of his life because he met the preacher whom they had been waiting to see and hear for a long time.

On one occasion on the way to Naqamtee, my husband was traveling all by himself and arrived at a village called Bakejaamaa. It was late in the evening, and he asked the people in the village to allow him to spend the night in their house. However, he was told that Qanyaazmatch Faranjii Boxxoo, the man responsible for overseeing the village at that time, gave an order not to allow any stranger to spend the night in their homes.

There were no hotels or inns in those days to spend the night when people traveled, so it was our custom to let strangers spend the night when traveling anywhere in Wollaga. Unfortunately, he could not find a place to spend that night because of the order given by the government official.

Finally, he turned around and found a little abandoned hut (godo) not far from the village. The hut was in bad shape, and there was a pile of ash in the center of the hut. He collected firewood from the surrounding area and made fire to warm himself and spend the night there. He did not know that the abandoned hut was where the hyenas reposed.

At midnight, as he fell fast asleep, the hyenas came from every corner and woke him up. He jumped up from his sleep and scared them away with his fire sticks and by throwing stones at them. Finally, the hyenas were scared of the fire and left him alone. He told us that he stayed up the whole night and did not go back to sleep until daylight. In the morning, he arrived at his destination and told the story of his ordeal to the church elders, who were waiting for his arrival. They let him rest for a day and continued his duty.

He wouldn't tell us all the scary things that kept happening to him as soon as he came home but waited a few months after the incident and shared it as a joke and laughed it off with everybody. Those types of incidents were so scary, but with God's help, all things were possible to bear.

I recall one time when he was coming from Yuubdo after preaching the gospel there. He and a boy who was with him had an encounter with a group of hyenas at night. They were between Yuubdo and Aira around Alfee River and were chased by hyenas. Luckily, they managed to escape by running to a nearby village. **Psalm 55:16: "But I call upon God; and the Lord will save me."**

There is a large and strong river called Birbir near Yubdo, Wollaga. My husband and the missionaries use to cross it by a rope before they built the bridge. They tied a rope over the river and walked over to across the Birbir river to preach the gospel. The risk was enormous but by the help of God they managed their work as it was planned.

One time on the way back from Europe his plane had an engine failure and it took him longer to get back home. He did not even have time to tell us about the incident when he arrived but we heard it from him later when he told it as a joke. His daily duty was focused on what God had planned for him.

How they crossed the Birrbir river

These are some of the many incidents I remember, but there were times that he faced rattlesnakes, lions, and tigers on his way to preach the gospel or on the way home. He often encountered bandits and robbers on the road while he was traveling, and they all let him pass safely without any harm, indicating to him that he was a man of God and that he was doing a good job. They knew he treated people's wounds and preached the gospel.

8

MOVE TO FINFINNEE FOR TRAINING

When Ms. Blair got back to Dambii Dolloo from Khartoum after liberation, she heard that I was raising the children all by myself because my husband was heavily involved in church work. This was the time when my husband, along with Luba Gidadaa Solan and Obbo Namarra Dheeressaa, went to Finfinnee for a court case and stayed there for eight long months to appeal their case of persecution by the Orthodox Church to Haile Selassie, and they had a very difficult time.

Every morning, people lined up on both sides of the road leading to the entrance of the Imperial Court of Haile Selassie to appeal their cases. When Haile Selassie arrived, everyone bowed their heads very low to greet him, and then he picked a few of them to step forward and present their cases to him.

It took them eight months to appear before him to present their cases even though they went there every morning. At the eighth month, realizing that the case was taking longer than they expected, they discussed among themselves what to do in order to get Haile Selassie's immediate attention.

They agreed to devise a plan that focused on Pastor Gidaadaa, who was blind. They encouraged Gidaadaa to remain standing while everybody bowed down when the emperor arrived in order to get his attention. Consequently, Pastor Gidaadaa remained standing when the emperor arrived while everybody bowed down, and the emperor asked why he was not bowing for him. They told him that he was blind.

The emperor ordered that he be brought forward and present his case. My husband and Obbo Namarra told the emperor's aide that they had the same case with Gidaadaa, and finally, they were able to present their case to the emperor.

Their appeals were to have their churches, which had been closed by the order of the lower courts, be opened for them and put a stop to perpetual persecution of Evangelical Christians in Wollaga. As a result, they got permission for their churches to be opened and for the Evangelical Christians to worship in their churches in freedom.

They returned home rejoicing.

Ms. Blair met with my husband in Finfinnee and demanded that she take me and the children from Aira to Dambii Dolloo to let me have some rest. At this time, the German missionaries had not come back after the second expulsion from Aira. It was at this time that the Swedish missionaries, who had returned, started helping my husband in the work that he was doing.

Reverend Stjarne the head of the Swedish Mission in Finfinnee, heard the news that Ms. Blair was complaining that I was bringing up three children on my own in those difficult conditions, and promised to bring our children and me along with my husband to Finfinnee to help me get some rest and to give my husband further training and put the children in school. We had three boys: Saamu'el, Paulos, and Girma, and I was expecting another baby, Hanna.

When we moved to Finfinnee, we brought four men with us, to also help them further their education. We brought along the two sons of Balambaras Disassaa Sibiilu Dheressaa and Tasfaa Disaassaa, Oljiraa Grany and Luba Taasisaa Dureesssa also came with us. Obbo Bayisaa Hoomaa came after we arrived in Finfinnee.

As soon as we got to Finfinnee, we asked Pastor Sharne to help us find a school for them. Having received the necessary education, these men returned to Wollaga. Some of them directly went to the pastoral training school run by Swedish Mission at Nadjjoo and later were ordained as pastors to serve the church.

Thanks to Reverend Stjarne of the Swedish Mission who moved us to Finfinnee for two years to help further my husband's education. At that time, Adde Naassise and her brother Obbo Baayisaa Fayyisaa, with their family, moved from Nadjjoo to Finfinnee, and we became one loving family. We called Adde Naassisee Harmee Naassisee (Mother Naassisee), and she helped me take care of our children during those two years we were together.

During my stay in Finfinnee, I used my talent that I received at Dambi Dolloo and taught some girls who were students at Etege Mennen School. Thanks to Adde Dinqinash Fayyisaa, the daughter of Harmee Naassisee, for introducing me to the students as she was attending Etege Mennen School.

I started teaching her different types of handcrafts, such as cross stitching, crocheting, and knitting sweaters. Dinqinash knew some handcrafts but wanted to learn from me how to use a variety of colors and a different style of work. Her friends Mulunash Ayele and Elfinash Wodaajo, the sister of Obbo Faasiil Wodaajo, came to our place with her to see my hand crafts.

One day, they told me that they had a competition at school and asked me to come up with a different style of handcrafts so that they could win. I taught them as much as I could, and they learned very well.

Elfinash Wodaajo applied for a handcraft teaching position, and she was asked if she had a different or variety of handcrafts that they had not seen before. I gave her what I had on hand to show them during the interview process so that she could pass the test to be accepted.

They accepted her, and she was so happy and thanked me by saying, "Long live Kanatu Karorsa!" She told me that she got what she had been wishing for a long time. She completely depended on me, and I had to help her in all the lessons that she would teach until she was able to get it all right.

That type of eagerness and dedication was a blessing. As for me, to help and see somebody grow is a joy of my life.

9

FROM FINFINNEE TO QAANNAO

Qaannao is my husband's birthplace. After my husband completed the two years of studies of theology and some academic studies in Finfinnee, the Swedish Mission moved us back to Wollaga to continue our work.

Before we left for Finfinnee, we hired a man called Obbo Dhufeeraa Dureesso form Caliyaa Ekkaa, who moved to the house where we used to live, to oversee the German Mission compound. Thus, we did not have a place to live upon our arrival from Finfinnee.

As soon as we came back, my husband's big brother Miijanaa Jammo insisted that we stay with him in Qaanna'o because he had lost his big brother Ofga'aa Jammo just before we returned. He did not want to live apart from his younger brother any more. They loved each other so much and started consulting and helping each other in so many ways.

His brother got his education at the Adventist Mission School in Gimbii Wollaga. When his big brother Miijanaa started building the Adventist Mission Station in Qaanna'o, my husband was unhappy because he wanted him to join the Lutheran Church. Unfortunately, that did not work out for them, so they both agreed to drop the case and move on even though a hot argument had developed.

The Reminiscence of Our Lives
In My Own Words

They favored their brotherly love, and both of them decided to respect and support each other in that situation. And they supported each other until death took them apart. Both of them did not put any kind of condition on their relationship, but they wanted to help each other without hindrance, holding on to what each believed.

I advise people around me to build that type of relationship and have love for each other regardless of differences. It was a very healthy and fruitful environment that they provided us to live in as a loving family.

My husband started going back and forth between Aira and Qaannao to build a house for us and build a new church in Waalgo Aira. As they promised us, the Swedish Mission from Nadjjoo followed us to Aira and asked my husband if he could build a temporary clinic next to our house on our own land.

"Now, my son, the Lord be with you, and may you have success and build the house of the Lord your God, as he said you would" (1 Chronicles 22:11).

They advised him not to build on someone else's land to avoid problems that may come as a result. He agreed and built the clinic next to our own house on our own land.

Meanwhile, a nurse named Sister Ingreed from the Swedish Mission rented a room from Obbo Turaa Guutee in Aira and started treating the sick people around Aira area until the clinic was built. She later moved to Caliyaa Ekkaa, where Balmbaras Gammadaa Urgeessaa lived, and traveled every Tuesday to Aira to help us out. Qaannao was between Caliyaa and Aira. I prepared lunch or dinner for her every Tuesday when she passed through Qaanna'o back and forth from Caliyaa to Aira. Those missionaries shared our burdens with us.

We lived in Qaannao for one year, and as soon as our house was completed, we moved to Waalgo Aira. We were very thankful to God for that kind of service and love we received from the Swedish Mission.

Rev. Daffa and Rev. Tasissa were among the congregations

The goal of our journey was not that we would do the work for God but that He would freely do His will to work through us.

We learned through all this that God has called us to His service and placed tremendous responsibilities on us. He expects no complaining on our part and offers no explanation on His part. God wants those of us who have an open heart and mind to do His work. He called us to do the things that we were perfectly fit to do by His grace, and that is where the cross we must bear will always lead.

10

CHURCH IN WAALGO AIRA

When my husband built the church in Waalgo Aira, the Aira government officials threatened to arrest him for building the Protestant Church. They told him not to build it and warned him that they would arrest him if he built the church.

His brother Miijanaa helped him build the church until it was completed. They built at night and slept during the day in order not to get arrested if they were found building.

The plan worked, and the whole church community participated in building it during the night. **"Blessed are those who have not seen and yet have believed" (John 20:21).**

Our church community became very strong and stood by us and supported us all the way to the completion of the building. Half the people watched for the police surrounding Aira, and half the people worked on the church with my husband, just like in the days of Nehemiah, when they rebuilt the wall of Jerusalem (**Nehemiah 4:21–23**).

The Rev. Daffa Jammo and Kanatu Karorsa in Aira Wollaga

The area police were so hard on us and kept watching my husband's steps and coming around my children to investigate where my husband was. I had a very hard time hiding my husband from our children because if they saw him, they would know what was going on with the church building. The good thing, at that time, was that since their father was always traveling, they just assumed that he was away traveling.

Thanks to our Lord and the community of Waalgo Aira for their dedication to stand with us at that difficult and dark time. None of them complained or showed us any negative attitude, only encouragement.

The primary opposition to us came from the Orthodox Church clergy and local government officials, such as Qenyazmatch Darasuu Waraabu. Qenyazmatch Darasuu threatened that he was going to hang my husband in the center of Gabba Facasaa (a local Tuesday marketplace) and hang Balambaras Gammadaa Urgeessa in the center of Gaba Gullisso.

My husband told him to his face that his thought was sinful and that was not good for him.

Balambaras Gammadaa sarcastically responded to him, saying, "Who kills who and expect to live in peace?" ("Eenytu eenyuun ajjeesee ofii immoo nagaan jirata?") "Please send him on my way."

Balambaras Gammadaa was accused of supporting the Protestant Churches in our area. Sure enough, he always stood by my husband and protected him from the area officials. We had a very respectful relationship with him. He strongly supported the education of the people and development of the area, and he was a very creative and innovative person who loved to see advancement of his Oromo people.

He supported the activities of both the German and Swedish Missions in the areas of education, health, and community developments in addition to the preaching of the gospel. He gave them land to build churches, schools, and clinics. He was the only progressive person with authority in the area at that time who built good roads and bridges all over the area, making it possible for people to travel from place to place without difficulty to do their business.

When Balambaras Gammadaa governed the area from Caliyaa Ekkaa to Nadjjoo, we were at peace, and our work was going so smoothly because we had Balambaras's voice to back us up.

One time, the opposition group from the Orthodox Church threatened to kill my husband when he traveled through Gulliso to Gimbii, and they planned to block the road to Gimbii. Some of our church group heard the rumor and went to check the area to find out if the rumor was true and rushed back to tell us.

My husband wrote a letter to Balambaras Gammadaa seeking his advice in this matter. Balambaras told my husband that he could go through his territory, where nobody would bother him.

So my husband changed his route and started traveling through Balambaras Gammadaa's territory. Finally, Balambaras went to the government authorities and warned them that if they took any wrong action against this man (my husband), there would be big consequences.

Balambarass Gamadaa Urgessaa and Rev. Daffa Diammo

After that, my husband and his helpers were able to travel without any difficulty to spread the gospel and build churches, clinics, and schools.

My husband faced a similar problem in Qellem Awraja, where Dajazmach Genene Badhaane was governor.

Genene emphatically said, "Unless Daffa was put to death, there would be no way that the Orthodox Church would survive in Wollaga Province."

One time, he sent an arrest warrant to my husband, saying that he had to go to Finfinnee to stand trial at the Imperial Court of Haile Selassie. In order to get to Finfinnee from Aira, he had to go through either Dembii Dolloo or Naqamtee. To go to Naqamtee, he had to pass through Guliso and Gimbii, a dangerous route. One of the area notables, Fitawrarii Riqitu, was also waiting on the way to abduct him.

This situation forced Dietrich Wassmann to decide to send him to Finfinnee through Dambi Dolloo. He took my husband to Dembii Dolloo, and Mr. Russell of the American Mission in Dembi Dolloo hid him in his house and bought him a plane ticket to Finfinnee.

On the next day, Russell dropped my husband off at the airport. My husband was surprised to see Dajazmatch Genene sitting in the plane when he entered. As soon as he found out that he was travelling with Genene on the same plane, he covered his head and face as though he was cold and passed him without being noticed and took the back seat behind him.

When they landed in Finfinnee, they saw each other eye to eye and greeted each other and went on their separate ways.

After two days, they met again at the court, and the case was presented to Haile Selassie's aide. Haile Selassie heard the case, and he told my husband that nobody had the right to arrest or kill him. He underlined the common saying "Religion is private, and country is collective." *Haimanot ye gil new hager ye gara new.*

Rev. Spings, Obbo Namarraa Dheeressa, Rev. Daffa Jammo and Obbo Baaroo Tumsaa In Nedjo

He told my husband that he was free to go back to his province and build as many churches as he wanted. This was a great victory for him and gave him a new strength to advance his ministry.

11

THE RETURN OF THE GERMAN HERMANNSBURG MISSIONARIES TO AIRA

My husband kept alive the dreams and the wishes of Louis Harms and Wassmann's teaching of the Lutheran doctrine by the grace of the Almighty God. The first Lutheran liturgy was introduced in Afaan Oromo in 1932 by the German Hermannsburg Mission in Aira.

During worship, the ordained pastor plays an important role in guiding and leading the liturgy. Everything was in a certain order, and the Lutheran liturgy book guides both the ordained and lay volunteer ministers to lead the worship service. All the church members know by heart the order of the liturgy.

This made and kept the unity of the church strong, and there was a strong love for one another among the believers. The goal was to remain true to the call of God and realize that His one and only purpose was to educate people to be the followers of God in accordance with the Scriptures. Thus, the core of my husband's ministry was to nourish the life of the believers and implant enduring love in their hearts.

Some years later, when the missionaries returned, they were amazed at the work. My husband had built several churches. The Swedish Mission played a big role in our personal lives as well as in building the church after the German Mission left, and helped us a great deal to do our work.

We progressed a lot with them. They loved my husband's dedication and eagerness to work without any hesitation. They recognized that he was looking for a better day yet to come, and one of the missionaries said, "That man is for the advancement of his people, and he gives his full attention to what he is doing. We need to help him and support him in his effort to spread the Word of God by all means."

He took care of schools, clinics, and churches, including the areas where the Swedish Mission started its work in Boodjjii, Nadjjoo, Mandii, and Naqamtee. By the time he retired, the church had grown to over five hundred congregations. Wherever he had been, there would be Christian baptisms, Holy Communions, weddings, and even burials, in case someone died upon his arrival. People did not have to wait for Sundays to hear the Word of God, and we never heard any complaining from church members about stopping their daily work to attend the church.

My husband, being the only pastor in the whole area at the initial stage, traveled a great deal on foot and by mule. They always looked forward to his arrival so that they could hear the Word of God from him. **"Blessed are those who hunger and thirst for righteousness, for they will be filled" (Mathew 5:6).**

Before his journey, my husband often sent a mailman before him to gather the people for him to teach them when he arrived. He would then teach them the entire week. Every day of the week became like Sunday. For example, our own second son, Paulos, was baptized on a Thursday. Even though I wanted our son to be baptized on a Sunday, it was my husband's duty and respon-

Mailman sent ahead of his departure

sibility to carry on his commitment to God. He told me that we are no better than the others, and he had to deliver what he heard, read, and understood from the Bible.

Every single day was programmed from Monday to Sunday, and his daily-routine life was just like that until the day he retired.

Since we truly decided to follow God, we had to go through every positive and negative thing that came our way. My husband understood what Jesus said. He heard it clearly, realizing the full impact of its meaning.

He did not go through life as a defiant person; he went through life with great determination and trust in God. His service was to pour his energy and ability out to the last drop for others. Praise or blame made no difference to him, for he understood that this world will perish but God's Word will abide forever. As I mentioned above, both of us had dedicated our lives to God in every possible way.

My husband's original salary was 3 birr a month, and after we married, it was raised to 5 birr. When the German Hermannsburg missionaries left for two years after the defeat of Italy, my husband was given the responsibility to manage the mission compound with about twelve workers. He was able to save about 200 birr from the water-powered grinding mill. However, the grinding mill broke down six months after the missionaries left Aira.

Two years later, Missionary Bahlburg, who was the head of the German Hermannsburg Mission at the time, came from Finfinnee and saw our work and how my husband responsibly managed the compound and honestly handled the money. Bahlburg asked my husband if they had incurred any debt to anyone for the operations of the grinding mill and the church, and my husband answered and told him that there was no debt at all. My husband then gave the key to Bahlburg.

Bahlburg was so amazed and told Reverend Wassmann that my husband was a faithful and honest man. In recognition of this fact, Reverend Wassmann wrote a short book titled *An Honest Shepherd Boy* detailing the sacrificial service of my husband. As a result, our salary was raised to 6 birr a month.

After the German missionaries left Aira, the Swedish missionaries came and learned about all the work we have been doing, and they raised our salary from 6 birr to 10 birr a month.

He carried the responsibility of spreading the gospel and introducing new believers to the Christian way of life, even in the absence of the missionaries. I was unhappy, but my husband told me that he was not working for the money but for the glory of God and to pave the way to eternal life for God's people.

My husband told me that the true testimony of my love for Christ Jesus was a very practical one and the rest is sentimental. My husband never complained about anything that came his way, but he always had a positive perspective. He cared about building a reputation of integrity so that the testimony for Christ Jesus would not be hampered.

One of my turning points was when I came to understand my husband's goal. I had convinced myself to be the breadwinner for my family, and when our family and community grew larger, it caused me to take serious action. I added the coffee farm to my daily work. I worked hard to pay the school fees, buy clothing, books and, in general, supported our family, including some in the community.

My husband's salary never came home at all. Whatever he got went to hospital fees and school fees for the needy. I am very thankful to God for giving me the knowledge to do all kinds of handcrafts so that I could use it for His purpose and His glory. I taught myself how to bead, make all kinds of artwork, and also taught our people so that they could teach others.

We raised our eight children on my income, and it helped us to spread the Word of God. When I started to work on the coffee plantation, the missionaries were unhappy with me, saying that we may forget God's work and follow the money.

I said to myself, *I lived and worked with them all those times to serve the Lord. How are they questioning my true belief in Jesus Christ?*

I told my husband that he should not get involved with our farm work but should continue concentrating on the business of the churches. I told him that I wanted to handle everything by myself around the house while keeping up with the church activities. I knew where my heart was, and I knew that nobody could show me the way to Him because I had already found my way to Him through Luba Gidaadaa Solan from my childhood.

Many people around the country knew my husband because of his work. Church members, teachers, and many others from all walks of life who came to Aira for many different purposes—medical, training, and church purposes—stayed with us since there were no hotels or guest houses in Aira in those days. The only person these people knew in Aira was my husband, so they all came to our house, and the burden of providing them with food and lodging fell on me and my children.

The money we received as a salary was barely enough for a couple of days to take care of all those guests. So I figured working on the coffee and fruit plantations was the only way to get some more income to take care of those guests, provide for their needs and our children's needs, and help my husband carry on his gospel ministry without worry.

Our children and I barely got a good night's sleep during all those days. It really took a toll on me and on my children. At times when I went to draw water from the river, I did not have enough strength to lift the water jar to put it on my back. I begged other women to help me lift it and put it on my back and asked my son Paulos to help me get it off my back when I got home. At times, I lost a lot of weight, and my legs started trembling so much that I could barely stand.

The missionaries noticed the toll the hard labor was taking on me. I was not sick, but very weak and exhausted. They persuaded me to take a break and regain some strength, so they took me to the new hospital they had just built and gave me a special room. They all took turns feeding me and took special care of me for two

With Wassman's family

weeks. I recuperated a little and got some more strength and got back to my hard work.

After a while, I got sick again, and I was admitted to the hospital for two weeks. Since I was still too weak to go home, Dietrich Wassmann (Dii Dii), whom I regarded as my oldest son, and Elze, his loving wife, took me to their home for two weeks and took good care of me until I recovered and got back to my work.

Looking back on my life, I realized how I came into a relationship with God by the help of the Holy Spirit through faith in Jesus Christ. Christianity is a willingness to submit to God's will with one's whole heart. I began to gain an intelligent appreciation and understanding of the wonder of the transformation in my life.

After the missionaries found out how determined I was, they backed off and started supporting me. Ditrich Wassmann started helping me transport my coffee to Gimbii and helped me to sell it.

If I had not worked that hard, there was no way that we could have raised our children and served the church. That coffee plantation supported our children, church, and our community.

Wassmann and his wife, Elze

A couple of times, the missionaries told me not to send our children to Finfinnee to further their education. They wanted Paulos to learn how to be a carpenter and for Hanna to be a dresser in Aira Hospital.

My answer to them was very short: "No." If it was for money, I was not going to ask anyone for help. I would rather take off my only clothes and sell them to support my children to further their education.

We decided that if our children wanted to advance their knowledge, we would support them by any means. We have never depended on anybody for our children's education. As I mentioned earlier, my handcraft work and work on the coffee plantation paid for our children's education, as well as contributions from my sister Elizabeth.

Paulos got scholarships through his efforts and through the help of Mr. Salsenburg in Germany. Our daughter Abby got scholarships through her effort and through Mekane Yesus and my sister Elizabeth and Pastor Gudina Tumsa, who helped guide her on the right path. Hanna got scholarships through her brother Paulos. The rest of our children depended on us throughout for their education.

Besides our children, we supported anyone who came to us for help and guidance with regard to education, and we did it from the depths of our hearts with the help of God.

We helped and guided so many of our young people to further their education. We did this by finding a way through the government and our missionaries to help advance the younger generation in education.

12

EXPANSION OF THE WORK IN COLLABORATION WITH THE MISSIONARIES

After the missionaries came back, our workload became larger than ever before. We wanted to educate the Christian girls we met at the new places we reached with the gospel. My husband invited all the girls from all over the area to come and stay for two months in Aira to learn how to cook, how to keep clean (hygiene), how to work on handcrafts, and study the Word of God every summer. We used our school boarding rooms, which were built by Dietrich Wassmann and Obbo Ciibssaa Dangalaa.

The church elders went from place to place to get the list of girls capable of learning and bring them to Aira to prepare them for training. These girls came from Gujji Getaaree, Ganijii, Babboo, Teggie, Caliyaa, Watto, Dannoo, Galaoo, Masinaoo, anad Kormee. My husband wanted us to teach all the girls from all the areas who had a connection with the church, as well as those who were not connected to the church in order to teach them the Word of God.

When the girls arrived in Aira, Ms. Kristal Rabin (the Aira school director) and I prepared the lessons to teach them. The lessons were very important and relevant for them. The main lessons were how to prepare butter with a variety of spices; stew (ittoo) in variety of ways; bread (budenaa); variety of spices; Oromo-style miimixa (hot pepper, jalapeno) with a variety of spices; and cooking lessons in general. We also taught them how to wash clothes, keep themselves clean, and organize their homes.

Ms. Rabin and I designed this project to help us in two ways. The first reason was that whatever we prepared in those two months would help feed the boarding school students for one year. The second reason was to help those girls to get an education in a practical way. Education was not encouraged at that time in our country in general, and it was rare for girls to have the opportunity to attend school.

Luba Taasisaa Dureessaa

This became a vital goal for my husband to accomplish during his leadership. He sat down and advised me by saying that if we could not educate our young generation, it's like we are hopping on one leg. He was so encouraged and enthusiastic when he laid down this program for me. I took it to my heart and executed the job as he instructed me to do.

Teaching handcrafts became very intense. The area women and girls were so eager to learn and wear new outfits and decorate their houses. I had great helpers such as Mrs. Ruth Sach and Mrs. Brulinde Baurochse. They played a big role in our women's lives, teaching them handcrafts, and at the same time, we shared the Word of God on Thursday afternoons.

Luba Taasisaa Dureessaa was engaged at that time to Adde Nuurituu Gettaa from Caliyaa Ekkaa, and she asked me to teach her handcrafts before their marriage. The only easy way to teach her was to send her a pattern, because she lived very far from me.

I prepared materials such as yarn and needles and started a design for her, like three or four lines of cross stitching, and attached the needle to the cloth and sent it to her. For sweaters, I did the same thing so that she could follow the pattern and make it herself. That way, it was easier for her to have an idea on how to go through the process.

When she got married, she moved to Aira, and it was easy to help her to advance. She was able to capture the idea quickly. She soon became our school handcraft teacher. I got a big relief and moved on to teach the community women and girls. **"My heart took delight in all my work (Ecclesiastes 2:10).**

Dr. Elizabeth Knohe, a medical doctor, and I started traveling wherever she was given a medical assignment. I traveled with her and gave handcraft lessons for women and young girls. We went as far as Gujii Getaaree, Ganjii, Caliyaa, Teggie, and many other places where the doctor was assigned.

The church leaders from all over the area organized their communities and encouraged them to join us to learn and get medical treatment. We told ourselves that we must avoid being selfish, hopeless, and careless and showing spiritual weakness. At that time, if we had not worked hard and seen the benefit of our work, we would have been just like a seedless tree.

Finally, I became an expert at growing varieties of vegetables, fruits, and flowers and produced numerous new hybrid plants over the years. One time, we counted thirty-eight varieties of vegetables, fruits, and flowers around our house. Some were brought from France, some from Germany, some from Sweden and America. Anything I planted bore good fruit. I was so delighted and encouraged to plant more. When I did that, it helped me to plant more seeds of hope and faith in our people's heart through the Word of God as well.

The Addis Ababa University advanced botany class requested an extended visit to my garden. They marveled at what they observed. I was encouraged even more. Even though our home was the center of church activities, our residence was known in the surrounding region as the House of Beads and Fruits. People from the neighboring areas who travel through Aira Village would ask for directions to our home in order to see my handiwork.

I enjoyed teaching and sharing my knowledge to whoever wanted to profit from my work. God never asked us to do anything that was naturally easy for us, but through His grace, we were perfectly fit to do these things. That is where I found my strength, and I was filled with joy by sharing the talent that God had given me.

As I mentioned before, my work was not limited to doing one thing only. I was fully involved in the activities of my community as needed. My husband was on the road most of the time. The government and the Orthodox Church had a strong relationship, and they did not approve of the expansion of Protestant Churches in the country.

One Sunday morning, as soon as I arrived at church, somebody informed me that about fifteen of our people had been arrested by three police officers to be taken to Gullisoo, the nearest government office.

I jumped out of my chair and followed them to where they were taking our people. They were about thirty minutes' walk from the church, and I caught up with them.

I asked them, "What did these men do wrong?"

The policemen told me that they did not show up for work. They kept on skipping work on Sundays because they preferred to go to church.

I demanded for their release, and I screamed until I could not hear myself anymore. I wanted them to be released immediately, and I told them to charge me or to take me with them. They turned around and looked at me and told me that they could take them with me but that they would report that I was disobeying the court order.

I told them to do whatever they wanted, but all I knew was that those people could not skip the church service. Finally, with God's help, I won my case and marched back to my church with my people with great victory.

13

FORMATION OF GIMBII AWRAJA BOARD (LATER EECMY WESTERN SYNOD) AND APPOINTMENT AS PRESIDENT

The (EECMY) Ethiopian Evangelical Church Mekane Yesus Western Synod was composed of all the Evangelical Lutheran Congregations in Gimbii, from both the German Hermannsburg Mission and the Swedish Evangelical Mission work areas, namely Aira, Caliyaa, Boodjjii, Najjoo, Mandii, etc. It was constituted in 1959 as a united body under one administration. My husband was elected as the first president to run the work of the board, and he faithfully served for twenty-five years in this position.

As president of Ethiopian Evangelical Church Mekane Yesus Western Synod, he attended both national and international meetings representing EECMY Western Synod. In 1952, he attended the second general assembly of the Lutheran World Federation in Hanover, Germany, as an observer representing his constituency. After the meeting, he visited Germany, Sweden, Norway, and Denmark and spoke to conferences about the evangelical movement in Ethiopia.

In 1955, he attended the first All-Africa Lutheran Conference held in Marangu, Tanzania. He was one of the founding signatories when the Ethiopian Evangelical Church Mekane Yesus was constituted as a national church in 1959, the EECMY Wester Synod being one of the four founding synods of the Ethiopian Evangelical Church Mekane Yesus.

When my husband became president of the EECMY Western Synod in 1959, we were in the middle of transition. We moved to our new home in Lalo Aira, and our children's demands were high. EECMY Western Synod asked my husband to move to Boodjjii, the headquarters of the Board. Boodjjii was far from Aira.

Things became more difficult to manage. I continued pushing things by myself while my husband was away from home. His work became demanding, and they hired Obbo Tasfaaye Darasuu to help him with office work and Obbo Namarra Dheressaa, a lawyer, to help him with legal matters.

My husband built a good relationship with both of them, and they had a strong bond. Both of these men had knowledge and wisdom, and they helped my husband a great deal.

As for me, the intensity of the work became overwhelming, and I had to prepare myself to manage both Aira and Boodjji homes with the help of God.

We were grateful to have good friends in Boodjjii who helped my husband when he moved there for his new job. Luba Djaallataa Waasee, Luba Namarraa Callaa, Obbo Galataa Boodjjii, and so many Christian friends helped my husband settle in the new location. They provided food and all the necessary things to make him comfortable and looked after him. They supported him in every possible way.

My husband had prepared himself to give spiritual nurture to the scattered groups of evangelical Christians in Central Wollaga, even before he was appointed as president. Spiritual awakening, which was started earlier, was intensified and gained momentum after the liberation from the Italian rule.

My husband traveled widely within his large parish, which contained several congregations, and built a good relationship within the Christian communities. It was not new and difficult for him to do the job. It was just a magnificent transition that was delightful to him to advance.

"Therefore go and make disciples of all nations" (Mathew 28:19). Teaching and watching the growth of his people was one of his dreams.

My husband allowed nothing to keep him from his deep conviction and true connection to the will of God. Every time he prepared to preach, he made sure that he was doing the will of God. A true Christian servant is one who permanently connects to God and then shares what he has received from God with others.

My husband never turned back or showed any doubt or expressed any weakness, but he grew closer to God all the time. That was how he was able to guide our lives and led us forward in our service to the church and the public. His deep desire was to introduce God and His Word to every human being who had not heard the gospel of salvation until there was no one left.

He never held anything in reserve; he poured himself out, giving the best that he had, and always stood by his words and actions. He felt responsible for any lost soul out there, and he did not want to leave any stone unturned. This was done out of his love for God.

One of his dreams and wishes was to see a theological college established in Aira. He fought a hard fight to do so. He wanted the college to be called Onesimos Nassib Theological College in memory of Onesimos Nassib, the translator of the Bible into Afaan Oromo. His dream was realized when the school was inaugurated.

At the inauguration, my husband started his speech with the following words: "What we heard by our ears, is what we see now by our own eyes [Guraan kan dhageenye, ijaan bira geenye], and all is for the glory of the Lord."

He finished his speech by saying, "People will no longer suffer traveling long distances to attend theology school or nursing school."

All he wished and dreamed for his people was not far anymore but was there in front of them.

He said in Afaan Oromo, "Wantaa kuunnoo jennee amma kunoo jennee."

He concluded, "This is the work of God."

14

LIFE DURING COMMUNIST TURMOIL

The story I am about to write is about the difficult experiences faced by the people of Oromo during the communist regime in the country.

The communist regime took over the government in 1974 by declaring "land to the tiller," which actually ended up being "land for the government." That was the darkest and hardest time of our lives, which I remarked as our challenging and trial times.

1. Detaining our pastors and healthcare specialists
2. Closing our churches
3. Closing our schools
4. Robbing each other and bringing each other down
5. Creating total chaos in our community

All the above-listed problems were in my mind as times of darkness and madness in our lives. I understand that many historians have written books on the communist military regime in our country, but my focus will be on the accounts and experiences we faced in our own small community.

When the madness started, the regime aimed at detaining some of the government officials and relatively all well-to-do individuals, whether they were law-abiding citizens or not.

The situation changed so fast that they started arresting, imprisoning, torturing, and killing any layman who was uncomfortable with a lot of the chaos created in the community.

They were determined to destroy our accomplishments of so many years but with the power of our Lord we have never put our heads down but looked up and forward for brighter days to come. The development we managed to build for our communities for years was down by our own community that we have built.

The volume of work we did for our community was enormous and amounts to the work of our lifetime, which may lead us to a brighter day.

There seems to be jealousy and meanness by the less well-off people against the relatively hardworking and well-to-do individuals. All these caustic environments were due to the turmoil brought to the country by the government. At that time, our people were not well educated enough to understand and evaluate what was about to occur and they were not aware that ignorance, the enemy of humanity, had taken over. All that happened was unfortunate, and those who planned this chaos gradually vanished out of our sight with the help of our Lord.

As the war broke, the chaos started, and propaganda started spreading around in everyone's ears, and those mobs started advising one another against the landowners and owners of better homes.

As I have noted earlier in this book, all that had been built were by my handcrafts and hard work with the talent that the good Lord has given me. I have never used my husband's salary as all his income went to school fees and hospital bills for the needy.

One day, some people whom we supported and raised came to our home and told me that my husband and I had enjoyed highlife enough already and told us to give up all our coffee land and fruits to the government. The young men we raised turned into a mob by the government, entered our home, checked our belongings, and interrogated us about where we got this and that. It truly hurts to talk about these petty things, but I have to record it in this book to tell the story of what happened to us in our lifetime.

My blood pressure went too high out of anger, and I got seriously sick and ended up in the hospital. I remember that the missionaries were worried that I could not be able to make it through, so they called my sister Elizabeth from Finfinne, called our children from where they were, and also our son Samuel from Massawa to come to Aira to see me before anything had happened to me. I stayed in Dr. Kritchman's home so that he could observe me day and night for about two weeks. Thank God I made it through that time. Harassments continued to agitate and distract us from all our activities during those days.

One time, they told me to make three blankets in a day for the auction so that they could make money off it. They warned me that if I didn't obey their orders, they would confiscate my sewing machine from me and put me in jail. At this time, they have already confiscated our coffee land, grain grinder machine, and orange and mango trees and gave them to the peasant associations. If we harvested one orange or mango fruit from our trees, we were told that we would be put in jail. The people who were harassing us were those whom we raised and helped by my handcrafts and those who ate from my fruits and also from my table. The militias advised my own family members, who we raised, to come home and kill me. I do not enjoy telling these stories, but all that happened at that time must be told because it was part of the story of my life.

At that time starvation took place and we did not even have coffee to drink. We ended up buying our own coffee drink from the peasant association. It looked as though the government wanted all of us to be very poor. Those who were better off before managed through somehow, but those who did not have anything before suffered even more. They were the ones that, however, were very mean to other people the most. At the same time, we were helping them through all these trying times.

In those days, the government did not actually attempt to control the land, but the approach was to open the floodgates of rural discontent, allowing the peasants to take over the land and encouraging them to organize into peasant associations. Sure enough, the peasants took the law into their own hands, distributed the land among themselves, and started robbing their own members or entering collective forms of land cultivation. The peasants aimed to nationalize the land as fast as they could to own anything they could get but could never know how to manage it and remained very poor. So anyone who owns a piece of land or toiled with his own hands to get some money with his own sweat without hurting anybody and contributing something to the development of the society which was doomed to be feudal and condemned to commit a crime, therefore, must be put to prison or even death.

The militia started to detain pastors, landlords, and German physicians (caregivers), leaving the community to be in turmoil. They put my husband and Obboo Gragnye Rooroo (the district chief of Aira) in prison. The militia told my husband that he was one of the feudal, so he must go to prison. They shackled their left and right legs together and put them in a small room, and they took them both to the market center called Gabba Jimaataa to shamefully display them around, telling them that the two feudal lords from Aira were captured.

Both of their legs got infected, and they were denied medical attention. I had a first aid kit from home and begged them to take care of them. They were both elders who were forced to be put in a small flee and lice-infected dark room without air inlets and to sleep on a small straw mat on hard ground. The small room was very hot, and the window and door were closed tight. Every morning, when I took breakfast for them, I found sweat dripping from them in a small dark room. Obbo Gragnye used to ask me to come to the prison very early in the morning to let them open up the window for them to breathe fresh air. What amazed me was that those two men never condemned and complained about their imprisonment because they well knew they did this to them out of ignorance, though I complained about their suffering for a long time.

I was so sad to see when our hardworking German physicians, caregivers, and nurses were mistreated. There was no law in order, no respect, and no appreciation for those missionaries who left their own luxurious life and gave their time and life to serve us during that dark time. Irreversible damage was done by our people. I hope and pray that this type of chaos will never happen again.

The Derg approached the established churches for the winning support and got them under its control and at the same time it was pitting the teachers, students, and peasants against the churches and pastors. Distributing church lands was widely approved; atheism and attacks on church dogma and practices and pastors were abhorred by the conservative peasants.

As church officials acknowledged, the Derg knew that the people followed their religion, and if it opposed the church directly, people would oppose the Derg, but at the same time, the Derg undermined the church religion indirectly and directly at times, creating more confusion within our community.

At this time, our friend Adde Nurituu Geetaa, Pastor Tasissa Duressa's wife, and I well understood what was about to take place, and we became strongly well prepared for anything coming our way to oppose the Derg's plan and protect our church community. Few students and teachers started mobilizing our community against us, but most of them stood by us and supported our plan. A few of those who were able to steer the problems left and right against the followers of Christ were even able to close the churches and schools in our area with the help of government militias.

They organized mobs, sending messages to our homes not to go to church on Sundays. Nurituu and I decided not to accept any orders from any one of them and started working underground, sending the opposite messages to our communities to attend the church. A couple of women brought the message to tell me not to attend church, and my answer was very simple to them. I asked them if they accepted Jesus Christ as their Savior, and they both answered me they had accepted Him. Then I told them to go away from my sight and to mind their own business. I have boldly told them that they have no authority over me to tell me not to go to church. That gave us a solid, strong ground to push them away. We both were well prepared to reject the proposal of their determination to interrupt our community. We mobilized our community every Sunday to leave home and hide in the garden or cornfield until I started walking to the church and then following me.

On my way to church, one of the militia followed me and asked me where I was going, and I told him that today was Sunday and told him to follow me to church. He could not dare to answer me back but turned around and went away. Nurituu prepared small sticks and rocks so that we could carry them in our packets to fight them physically with God's help. The good thing is that there was a pile of small rocks collected by our church at that time, which was prepared to remodel our church.

We managed to grab them in our hands to fight them back. We did not have any guns, but we were well prepared with the help of God to use those rocks and sticks to challenge them because all things are possible with God. As our group saw me entering the church, they all came in with me and entered the church. A couple of the militias came in and asked me what I was doing in the church, and I told them, "Today is Sunday, and you sit down and wait for a pastor to come and preach."

He did not say a word but left the church premises.

I thank Addee Nurittuu Gettaa for her efforts and contributions to the Aira community during that dark time. She was a very intelligent and an alert leader who we had among us. She managed to guide and mobilize our Christian women without fear but marched forward with our plan to diminish the Derg's power as much as we could. All glory be to our Lord for pulling our community out of that troublesome time, and I am grateful for our underground supporters.

15

MY HAND CRAFTS WORK

Rev. Daffa Jammo and I

The Reminiscence of Our Lives
In My Own Words

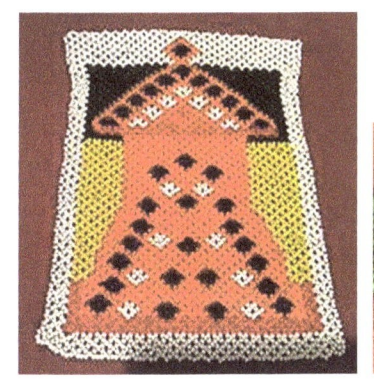

Rev. Daffa Jammo and I

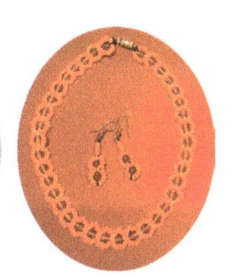

The Reminiscence of Our Lives
In My Own Words

79

Rev. Daffa Jammo and I

THE REMINISCENCE OF OUR LIVES
IN MY OWN WORDS

**Displaying my
beads work**

**Rev. Daffa was watching how
I do a new design.**

In front of our house in Aira Wollaga

Beading

Hand made outfit   Teaching children how to garden

Working in a garden   Flowers in front of our home

The Reminiscence of Our Lives
In My Own Words

Our mongo tree

Teaching my children how to garden

16

FAMILY AND FRIENDS

The first Lutheran church in Aira Wollaga Wassmann built 1952. I think the top of the church represents the 12 disciples.

Rev. Daffa after Ordination.

THE REMINISCENCE OF OUR LIVES
IN MY OWN WORDS

Rev. Daffa arrived in Germany 1952.

Rev. Daffa on the way to Germany

Rev. Daffa in Germany

Rev. Daffa on the meeting in 1952 in Germany.

Obbo Dheresaa Bato, Obbo Lamu Simaa & Rev. Daffa Jammo in Aira

Rev. Daffa in Germany.

Rev. Daffa showing cultural game to the students in Germany.

THE REMINISCENCE OF OUR LIVES
IN MY OWN WORDS

Rev. Daffa in Germany 1952

Rev. Daffa & Kanatu With Wassmann in Germany.

Rev. Daffa infront of our church in Aira.

Rev. Daffa Jammo and I

Rev. Daffa & Kanatu with
D. Wassmann in Germany.

Rev. Daffa & Kanatu
with Wassmann.

Rev. Daffa addressing the OAU.

THE REMINISCENCE OF OUR LIVES
IN MY OWN WORDS

Ato Emanuel Abraham, Rev. Daffa Dajammo & Fit. Bayessaa Jammo in OAU meeting

Celebration 50th anniversary 1986.

The two sisters, Kanatu, & Elizabeth Karorsa

Elizabeth & her husband Capt. Tessema Eranaa.

Rev. Daffa Jammo and I

Obboo Fajii Karorsaa.

Elizabeth & Kanatu with the family

Family in Aira infront of our house.

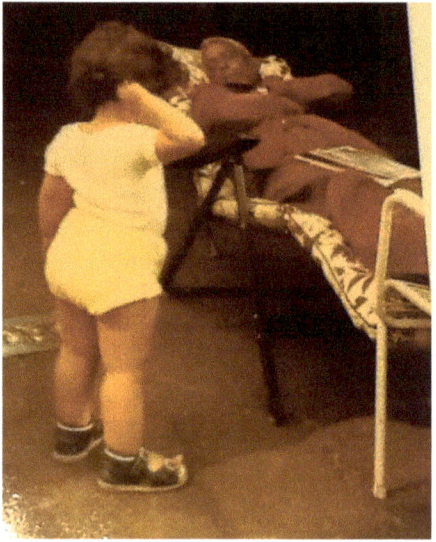

Baby Genet scared to wake up grandfather Daffa.

The Reminiscence of Our Lives
In My Own Words

Best friends Dani & Eliz.

Family 1984 in Dallas Texas with
Obbo Abraham Mamoo

Obbo Gutama Rufoo, Luba Terfa Jaarsoo, Mrs.
Elizabeth Karorsa & Rev. Herald Kurtz

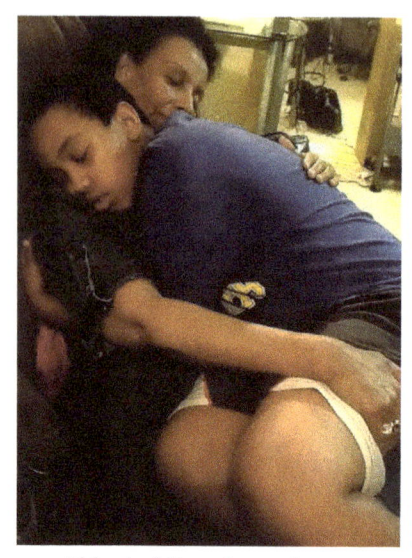

Abby holding sleepy Logan

Abby, Nate, Boenna, and Kebron

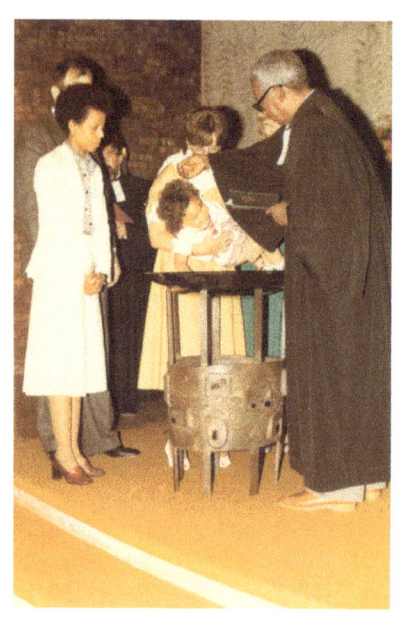

Baptizing his granddaughter in Germany in 1984

Boenna with his grandmother

The Reminiscence of Our Lives
In My Own Words

Deribee with her husband and son Logan

Deribee and Kanatu

Rev. Daffa Jammo and I

Dani, Hanna, Abby Tsion, and Rev. Manfred Zach after our brother Paulos funeral in 2007

Elizabeth and Tesemaa in 1992, last time they were together in Minnesota

Elizabeth, Tsion, and Anu on Deribe's graduation

Elizabeth and Abby, 1983

Elizabeth in First Presbyterian Church in Wichita, Kansas, 1980

Elizabeth with grandchildren.in 1993

The Reminiscence of Our Lives
In My Own Words

Ejersso Dawit and his family

Elizabeth, Kanatu, Abby, Tsion, and Deribee

Forever best freinds Tsion and mother

Girma, Daniel, Berhanum Solan, and Ayanos.

Rev. Daffa Jammo and I

Family prayer time

Family at Logan's graduation, 2019

Hanna, Abby, and Deribe

Kanatu and Abby on Nathan's graduation in 2008

Kanatu and Dani

Kanatu & Abby on Kebron's graduation in 2010

The Reminiscence of Our Lives In My Own Words

Hanna Daffa

Kanatu and Abby

Kanatu and Sam

Kanatu and Tsion, best freinds forever

Rev. Daffa Jammo and I

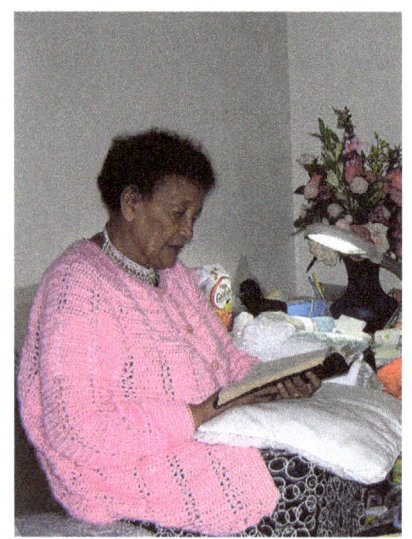

Kanatu reading her Bible

Kanatu reading her Bible at age 97

Kanatu, Sam, and Nathan

Kanatu, Abby, and Tsion

The Reminiscence of Our Lives
In My Own Words

Kanatu with family on Kebron's graduation with the family members 2010

Kanatu and Deribee

Rev. Shiferaw with his family

Obo Tasfayee Deresuu was with us at Oromo Lutheran Church in Dallas, Texas, 2016

Tsion and her husband, Hakeem, with Kanatu

Tessemaa and Abby in 1992

Martha Mijana with her mother; husband, Obbo Baniti Detii; and her family

Magree and Mitiku Waaqoo's family

Mother's Day celebration at Oromo Lutheran Church in Richardson, Texas

The Jammo and Waqo's family

THE REMINISCENCE OF OUR LIVES
IN MY OWN WORDS

Sisters forever: Kanatu and Elizabeth

Tsion with Elizabeth and Tesemaa Erenna

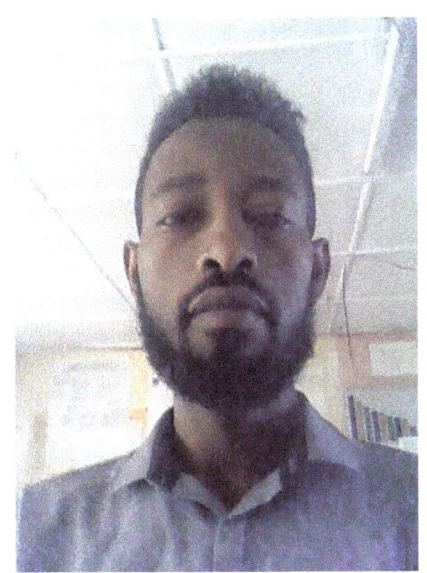

Lemessa Dawit

Simbatu Nagarii

17

LEGACY

1. My husband strongly opposed the government's restriction of use of various languages, specifically Afaan Oromo, other than the Amharic language in Oromo land, with regard to the Word of God and preaching of the gospel. Our people were not introduced to modern education at that time. His philosophy was that a child never knows what it means to walk at birth but that he or she learns how to walk after months and learns how to jump after that.

    The implication of this saying was that a mother tongue has priority over other languages. After someone learns their own language well, then they will be able to tackle other languages. Thus, the understanding and respect my husband showed for our language, Afaan Oromo, during those dark days, was remarkable.

    When the announcement came from Haile Selassie's government, Wassmann and my husband were amazed and started asking each other about it. Wassmann was puzzled to hear that Amharic was mandatory since the people were Oromo. My husband said it was an insult to force a different language on our people since we had the gospel in Oromo, and he asked why they were forcing our people after we had already put everything in order.

They quickly decided that was totally unacceptable and they were not going to implement it. However, the Swedish Mission at Nadjjoo, Boodjjii, Mandii, and Naqamte complied and demanded that people should obey and learn Amharic and the mission continued using Amharic as the medium of teaching. That was not acceptable to our people.

2. My husband had such a great determination to learn German language. He had not been able to learn enough from Wassmann that much before the war started and the Germans were told to leave Ethiopia. Wassmann left him a small German dictionary and told him that when he come back he will continue teaching him, and my husband was dedicated to teach himself every word with its meaning. He was not even sure that he would be able to use it in the near future.

I asked him why he tried so hard to learn German when we didn't know when the German missionaries would return. He told me that he would never give up, that God would bring the German missionaries back some day, and that he would be able to use it again. Even though they told us that they might be back, we were not sure because the country's situation was in chaos at that time. Anything could have gone wrong, but he was so hopeful that God could bring the best out of the worst.

3. He was determined to request for medical doctors, nurses, and teachers from Germany to come to open schools and hospitals in our country. Sometimes he faced difficult situations, but he always had a solution. Once they told him that they have already sent enough doctors, nurses, and teachers. He answered by putting his hand on his head and showing them in a dramatic way that he was not requesting them to bring his people up to their own standard but he was trying to make their lives a little better. By doing so, he got their attention and got his wish of more doctors, nurses, and teachers for Wollaga Province to open schools, hospitals, and build churches.

4. One time, my husband requested a car for western synod for transportation, and he was told by the general assembly meeting that they wouldn't allow western synod to have a car for their

work. Their excuse was that there were not enough cars whereas they had a variety of transportation in Finfinee, such as buses and taxis. Yet they wanted to have more cars for Mekane Yesus headquarters.

In the middle of the general assembly, Reverend Lundgren asked him, "Pastor Daffa, weren't you traveling by mule before? Why are you requesting to get a car for the synod now?"

He replied, "Before, all of us were asleep and did not have any options, but now we are all awake and we have to walk a talk."

He strongly emphasized that what had happened before would never happen again in his lifetime, and that he needed to see his people's advancement in every angle and move faster to spread the Word of God. My husband wanted to do more for his people to enhance their living standard. His determination resulted in the approval to get more cars for the western synod for church work.

5. When we were in Laaloo Aira, a man named Amanu, who lived with Obbo Turaa Guutee, asked my husband to take him to Finfinnee to buy a sewing machine. My husband took him, and he purchased the machine and came back with my husband to Aira. However, the man did not know how to sew, but my husband's understanding was that he knew how to sew. On another trip to Finfinnee, my husband purchased three pieces of clothes—pants, a coat, and a shirt—and asked that man to take them apart one by one so he could learn from it. My husband showed him how to take them apart very carefully, and the man did as he was directed so he could learn how to sew clothes.

On the next trip, my husband bought women's and children's clothes and did the same thing. That man used that as a pattern and learned how to sew. We also taught Obbo Shuramo Ujukaa how to sew. After that, the Aira community no longer needed to travel far distance to purchase clothes. One time, I sent Obbo Alamu Nagarii to my brother in Dembii Dolloo to learn from him how to cut and sew clothes.

These are just a few of the many things that I am reporting to help the younger generation understand how we came to this bright day. This was the way my husband and I guided our people to the bright future.

18

OUR CHILDREN

We were blessed with nine children and eight grandchildren. Our children's names are Ayyaantuu, Samuel, Paulos, Girma, Hanna, Abby, Daniel, Tsion, and Diribee. Most of our children were born in Aira. Our grandchildren are Solan, Aayanos, Eillily, Nathan, Boenna, Kebron, Genet, and Logan.

Three of our children—Ayyaantuu, Paulos, and Hanna—have gone home to be with the Lord. They are greatly missed, and we believe they are in the good hands of our Lord.

Besides our children, we raised ten children who had lost their fathers. Even though their mothers were around, we helped raise the four children of Obbo Bulchaa Leelloo, who was a guard of Aira Hospital. He suddenly became sick and died in our hospital.

We also helped raise six of Obbo Abdiisaa Baacaa's children. He died of short-time sickness, and both widows asked us to take care of their children. We fulfilled our promises and took care of the children as our own children under their mothers' supervision.

We had over fifty-seven students in our own home and put them through school at different times. Some of them came to us to get treatment at the hospital and stayed with us for school. Some of them came to us just to get education. A couple of them came from far away, escaping from their captors who were going to sell them as slaves. We hid them in our house and taught them the Word of

God. Some of them became preachers or teachers. The success was a triumph for them as well as for us.

Besides the fifty-seven students, we also adopted a young boy by the name of Barrii Bultum at age seven. Barrii's mother had two sons and decided to give Barrii to us and his big brother Guyaa to my husband's big brother.

Barrii helped around the house the same way our own children did, and they all had their share of chores. Barrii was married to Jabanee Tollaa, and they had ten children, and eight are still alive. We raised them all as well. They helped us raise our children, and they were the center of our lives and have done an excellent job in helping us in our journey of Christian life.

Barrii traveled with my husband and accompanied him to spread the Word of God during those dark days. Barrii and his wife, Jabanee, passed away just two years apart. Both were greatly missed by our community of Aria and my family. We are very grateful to God for the life we shared.

Obbo Barrii Bultum

One of the girls we raised was Birqee Habaku. I taught her reading and writing. After she learned how to read and write, she went back to her parents.

One early morning, Birqee came back to our house. My husband asked her why she came. She replied that she needed the Holy Bible because she was ready to teach the Word of God. He jumped out of his chair and said that he just found a person who could help him with teaching. He gave her his own Bible, blessed her, and sent her back to the village where she came from. He promised her that he would come in a week's time to see how she was doing. He went as he promised. Today, that village has become a Christian community and has its own church.

We thank Adde Birqee Habaku for her service to her community and for the life that she shared with all of us. She was such a trustworthy person, and we all enjoyed being around her. She went home to her loving God.

All the credit goes to God for His help in raising our children.

I also would like to express my gratitude to my younger sister Elizabeth and her husband, Captain Tessema Erena. Elizabeth and Tessema played a big role in our children's lives. If it were not for God and them, we would not have been able to raise our children at all. From the day our first child, Ayyaantuu, was born, up to the last baby, Deribe, they shared their entire lives with me and my family. I thank the Lord for both of them for sharing their lives with us.

When we were unable to pay the school fees or buy their clothes, they were there to cover it all. They were our backbone. We greatly miss both of them.

My sister traveled to America back and forth to further her education and for church meetings from her young age, and she bought fashionable outfits and shoes for me and my children every time she came home. However, I did not want to wear the outfits my sister bought for me because they were too fancy for our community. I did not want to look different from the rest of my people. I wore those outfits whenever I visited my sister in Finfinnee. It feels good when we all look alike in our community.

Our own children shared our burdens with us. Samuel helped us for a short time because we sent him to Nadjjoo for school at a very young age, but when he came home, he worked with his brothers Paulos and Girma and his sister Hanna.

After Abby, Daniel, Tsion, and Deribe were born, we had some help from our neighbors and from the students who lived with us to attend school. They helped with washing feet, making beds for the guests, cutting grass for the mules, fetching firewood, drawing water from the river, cleaning the house, and helping me prepare breakfast, lunch, and dinner.

Paulos and Girma

The Reminiscence of Our Lives
In My Own Words

Specifically, Paulos, Girma, and Hanna paid a big price with us. They worked so hard, and they did not have time to study but ran here and there to help us out in every way possible. Hanna helped in the kitchen, and Paulos and Girma helped with the guests and cut grass for the mules and washed feet or prepared a place for the guests to sleep.

Paulos and Girma also helped Hanna in the kitchen by cutting onions for stew, cutting greens, and starting a fire to make bread (budeena). They helped her because she was small, and they especially helped out if I was sick or after I delivered babies until I got strong. Our home was full of work and full of guests.

Our first son, Samuel, as I have mentioned above, left home at age nine to Nadjjoo for his elementary studies. Whenever he came home, he did his share of any given work. After completing his schooling in Nadjjoo, he went to the evangelical college in Bishoftu and the General Wingate School in Finfinnee and Haile Selassie University.

Samuel Daffa

He later joined the naval college in Massawa and earned his degree as a naval officer. He gave a great service for his country as a naval officer, and when Haile Selassei's government was overthrown by the military (the Durge) in 1974, he left the country and ended up in Germany, and joined the university and studied fine arts. He later moved to the United States and now resides here.

I want to share a short story about two of our sons, Paulos and Girma. They were very thoughtful, loving, humble, and caring young boys and worked hard with us. They loved their community in which they grew up. Especially Paulos loved to gather the young boys of the community to teach or to tutor them.

Every summer, they worked on different projects for the community. There was a committee within the community called "Wayyessaa." This committee included all age groups and made a connection with those in authority in the area to get permission in order to do things for the betterment of the community. By doing this, they gained the support of those in authority in the area, such as Qenyazmatch Darasu Waraabu, Obbo Grany Roroo, and Balambaras Dheeressaa Sibiluu.

The strategy was to open the communication within the community and the neighboring villages so that they can travel freely to markets and do their daily work. They had noticed that there were many people who lost their lives by drowning in the rivers while traveling from market to market for business.

To solve this problem, they built bridges wherever needed to make the travel easier and safer. They also dug wells so that people wouldn't have to travel far to get water. All these innovative ideas emanated from the fourteen-year-old boys who accomplished a lot for their community.

One thing I admire about our son Paulos is that he included all ages so that the younger ones could help him when he was short of energy. The people younger than him learned to use his strategy in the near future.

When he planned the "Wayyessaa" project, he outlined the plan and set the committee with his brother Girma and friends Bichagqaa Fayissa, Elias Negassa, Obbo Tesfayee Darasuu, and Hundumaa Grangne.

After that, they added the members with the following groups: Olanii Hommaa, Margaa Fitee, Endaalu Lamu, Bantii Dhuferaa, Berhanuu Fajii, Barrii Bultum, Emaanna Bonayaa, Waqlataa Sardaa, Negesee Laloo, Mengesha Nagaoo, Saadraqe, and Amanuel Ashannaa.

He distributed the job among them, and he also allowed young students from age ten and up to follow him. Those young students were Daniel Daffa, Yosef Chibssaa, Negesee Kidanee, Daniel and Olqabaa Tessemaa, Negesee Lamu, Ragaa Sorrii, Bekumaa Galatee, and many more, including neighborhood young students. Even little kids like Tsion Daffa, Sarraa Dheresaa, Abebech Nagasaa, Feben Tasissa, Ebbissee Ashanaa, and Hundatuu Chalaa. These young students did their fair share as their ability and energy allowed them to do the job. Their small duties included collecting wood for those who were cooking for lunch at the field area, preparing coffee, and handing out water to drink.

Some of the girls who participated in Wayyessaa by cooking and feeding the participants were Aster Bato, Makadash Grangne, Buuranee Tessemaa, Hanna Daffa, Abby Daffa, Adde Zenebetch Darassu, Djalatee Chibsa, Mulunesh, Saraa Jorgoo, and others.

Especially, I thank the area selfless mothers who supported him by making and carrying the Budeenaa (bread) to their destination and coming to chaperone the young children. I also thank my brothers Fajii Karorsaa, Obbo Nagassaa Kittii and Obbo Jorgoo Seenoo, who never left our young students alone. They followed them everywhere they went to help and protect them in every way.

Paulos went to Germany to further his education, and Girma became a pharmacist by earning his bachelor of science in chemistry. When Paulos went to Germany, we wanted him to become a pastor, but his ambition was to be a farmer, and he did not have that pastoral inner call within him. We all understood that to be a pastor is a call of God. So we supported him to continue his studies in the field of agriculture, and he earned his doctoral degree in agriculture.

Dr. Paulos Daffa

As soon as he finished his studies, he wanted to come back and put into practice what he had studied to help the community he so loved. In the meantime, a military coup broke out and the country was in a mess. We told him not to come at that time, hoping a better day would come. Thus, he was not able to come home.

Our son Paulos died in Germany and never came back to live among the community he loved and served except for one short visit. We accepted his death as God's will and lived with it. May he rest in peace.

Hanna Daffa

Our daughter Hanna went through hard times with us serving us and our guests. Since she was the first daughter after Ayyaantuu, she had to play the role of a girl in the family. She helped in the kitchen starting at the age of five, and by age ten, she was capable of making bread and stew (budeenaa and ittoo).

It broke our hearts because she had so much work to do from a young age, but we did not have any other choice at that time as everybody in the house was busy doing their share. Since we had so many guests, she had to make coffee eight to ten times a day. Our house was always full of guests from left to right, and she was there for us, ready to help. My regret was that she did not enjoy her childhood days as much as her other sisters.

Brothers and sisters grieving Hanna's death in March 2016 in Germany

Saturday was a special workday for my children, and everybody had to be up at 6:00 a.m. to do the work. All of them knew their share, and we do not have to tell them what to do but just remind them that it was Saturday. Saturday was the day that we cooked and cleaned our front and back yards and worked in our garden. We had to prepare our home for Sunday, the Holy Day. We had to make our home presentable.

We had to go to the church and clean it in and out for Sunday worship service. On Sunday, nobody was allowed to work, except for setting the table for lunch and making hospital visitations. That was the only resting day we had in a week.

We did enjoy our Sundays with friends and relatives. We still served our guests, but we did not work in our garden, collect firewood, pound coffee, or cut the trees or grass. Of course, some of the congregation members came home with my husband and spent the afternoon with him whenever he was around. But we always served guests whether or not he was around.

The Reminiscence of Our Lives
In My Own Words

Working in the garden was not an easy job. Our house was built on hilly land and was barren. There was nothing in our lives that our children did not help with. Our children had to go around the cattle pastures and collect the dry dung for fertilization. It would be piled at one place and be pounded by heavy wooden sticks so that it could be placed on the garden fields before it rained. We had to dig the garden field and spread the dung inside the hole and cover it up with the soil that we dug. Hence, it wouldn't be flooded away from the field by the rain. If it wasn't raining, then our children would bring the water from the river and spray it all over our garden.

We also used donkeys to carry the water. After a couple of days, I had to plant flowers, fruits, and whatever was needed to be planted around that area.

That is how I made my garden fertile and was able to get good fruit out of it. Our children worked hard, but they did not enjoy eating those fruits as much us our neighbors because they left home to further their education. I feel bad about that, but all is well with me, for He gave me the energy and talent to share our lives with our community. These were part of the jobs that were heavy on our children. They were too little to understand how tedious the journey was that my husband and I took.

Mother and son Daniel Daffa

Once, our son Daniel complained about lack of sleep on weekends. One Saturday, I woke all of them up at 6:00 a.m. as usual, and he told me that it was our house, it was not a factory, and we need to get our rest and long sleep. That hit me, but I could not stop from waking them up to help me. I divided the work among them according to their age and level of their strength.

Daniel completed his elementary school in Aira and got his high school education at the Evangelical

College in Bishoftu. Upon completion of his studies at this level, he joined Haile Selassie I University.

While he was there, he got involved in politics and joined a student uprising when he was in his fourth year and was arrested and put in prison. He was imprisoned for eleven years.

My husband and I never spent holidays together after his arrest. We took turns every holiday traveling to Finfinnee to visit him in prison.

Since the unpredictable Communist ruler Mengistu Hailemariam was killing prisoners during the holidays, we made sure to see our son before anything happened to him. That was the toughest time that we experienced in the lives of our children. It was in the midst of all these difficulties that we raised and educated our children with the help of God the way we could and the way we knew how.

God is always good, and we got our son back. He joined his brother and sisters in the USA, continued his studies, and got his MA in Conflict Resolution. He now resides in the USA.

Our children missed their father a lot because he was always on the road, and they did not get a chance to see and play with him, like most kids do. Whenever he came home and had a little time to play with them, he would tell them short stories from the Bible and check their schoolwork. He would play a game with them around the fire, tell them fiction stories about animals, and play a variety of games such as *takkooyyee*, *lamooyyee*, *Ibboo*, *Tokkeen malii*, etc. He also wrote the children's play book.

Our daughter Abby told me that my husband and I had chosen the life of Mary and Martha from the Bible, and she caught me by surprise when she quoted, **"No one who put his hand to the plow and looks back is fit for service in the Kingdom of God"** (Luke 9:62).

My husband and I were very committed to serving our God. As I reflect back now, I see that one of the reasons that our children did not want to participate in church leadership or become pastors is that the life they shared with us had a great impact on them. They were terrified and thought that was the only way to live. We paved a way of life for the rest of the community but not for our children.

The Reminiscence of Our Lives In My Own Words

They convinced themselves to choose their own way. We did not blame them but supported them in any way they wanted to grow, as long as they attended church and had love, fear, respect for our God Almighty. We imposed education on them so that they could depend on themselves, not on anybody else. My husband and I told them so many times to keep the Word of God in their hearts and abide with it as long as they lived. Most importantly, we wanted to let our children know that the most important aspect of the Christian life is our personal dedication and relationship with Christ Jesus.

Specifically, I pushed our children toward education. I saw the importance of education when I was a little girl in Dembii Dolloo, watching the government beating uneducated, weak, and poor people and tying their hands behind their backs and taking them to jail for not working on the government officials' farms. When those in authority (the Nafxanyas) gave their mules to be fed by the peasants, they would measure the mule's stomach. If the mule's stomach was less full than earlier, that man would be beaten up and sent to jail.

Rev. Daffa and Kanatu

I was around seven or eight years old when I made up my mind to study hard to be a leader to protect the poor people. After I came to Aira, my husband was dealing with the same kind of problem, protecting the people around him because they did not know how to read and write in order to protect their right.

Also, I witnessed how the government officials, Orthodox priests of that time, abused our society. Whenever the farmers farmed spices such us peppers, onions, garlic, ginger, or any kind of grains, they sent their wives to check on our people's backyards or farms to see if the farm was ready to be harvested. If it was not ready, then they will order someone to watch the farmers so that they wouldn't harvest without their permission. If they were caught harvesting or picking or even broke one of the corns from their field, they would be put in prison.

The poor farmers' wives left their babies unattended under their storage (Gombissa, where they collected the grains) or under the shade of their house to go to those ruler's home and clean their yards, prepare food for them, and bring water. At the end of the day, the wives of those farmers collect their starved babies from wherever they left them in the morning. That is, if those babies made it through the day alive. There were so many dangers that happened. If they had enough energy, the wives cooked for their children and put them in bed.

As I was observing all these unfair things happening to those poor farmers, it hurt me and made me strong to prepare myself for the hard life. In my mind, I was crying to God and prayed, "If You give me children of my own, I promise to teach them to protect the poor and live a good life."

Those government officials and the Orthodox priest became the owner of the land and gave the full authority to themselves of Oromo land. Land is an important property with immense use by the owner; thus, that land must be used to carry on the owner's daily activities instead of activities by an outsider. At my young age, I felt this was injustice.

People at that time were scared to go to church because if the government officials found out they were going to church, they would accuse them of skipping a work day and arrest them. Therefore, my husband was involved in church and community cases all the time. He was appealing to those in authority to release those who were put in jail. The government officials were looking for excuses to arrest them to collect money from the poor, and my husband wouldn't allow that to happen. He went everywhere needed in order to have them released. At that time, I realized that my husband had become a voice for the voiceless.

As soon as we started having children, I told my husband that if we did not educate our children, they would be just like those uneducated people who were pushed around by officials or police. We advised our children to respect the Oromo culture and the law of the land in which they lived and helped them understand their rights, to express their feelings and their human dignity in ways appropriate.

In those days there were no good roads, no cars, no trains, no airplanes and no telephones. The pastors used to travel on foot or on mules to spread the gospel. The life of a family of a pastor was very hard and our children lived it first hand. In the twenty-first century people can travel as they wished and sarcastically, one of our children told me, "This is the time that everyone can be a pastor, but it wasn't that way when our father was a pastor."

I told our children that being an honest pastor is a call, and that call is a service to God with full commitment and dedication; it is not just a simple career or a luxury work. A person has to give his heart and life to God to be a pastor. True, many pastors have neglected to follow the example that Jesus has set for us but try to enrich themselves. That is not biblical at all.

19

HUMOROUS SHORT STORIES

A good friend of ours, Obbo Namarraa Dheeressaa, was a bright gentleman who was good at handling legal issues. He and my husband traveled from court to court together between Gimbii, Naqamtee, Yuubdoo, and Finfinnee to appeal or present any case that came on their way concerning the church.

One time, they went to Naqamtee to present their case to Dajazmach Fikreselaasee, the governor of Wollaga province, who loved to go hunting rather than appear in court to do his job. My husband and Namarraa stayed in Nakamtee for more than fifteen days just to see him, and they ran out of food and money that they took with them. Every morning Fikreselaasee came out of his house, they stood by his gates and saluted him, and he rushed away from them to hunt.

Namarraa told my husband jokingly, "Had we been a deer, Fikreselaasee would have paid attention to us very easily."

Reverend Daffa with Obbo Namarraa Dheressaa. Best friends.

The Reminiscence of Our Lives In My Own Words

Most of the time, the situation was very frustrating, but they joked and laughed off their anger.

At another occasion, when they were supposed to appear in court, Namarraa was a little late. My husband was called to present the case in the absence of Namarraa.

As soon as my husband started to present the case, Namarraa, all of a sudden, appeared in court. As he listened to my husband's presentation of the case, he was not satisfied. So he pushed my husband aside and started addressing the judge angrily. This made the judge disgruntled.

My husband leaned over and whispered in Namarra's ears, "Don't let the thunder come down on us but the cold rain."

He wanted Namarra to calm down so the judge wouldn't throw them out of court. Everybody at the court laughed, including the judge. The case was examined, and the judge dismissed the case in favor of my husband.

These types of things happened several times and became the talk and joke of the time.

On our way home from Finfinnee to Aira, Obbo Baayisaa Fayisaa and some of our people were with us to help us with the children. As soon as we passed Nakamtee, a person came to us with some bad news. The outlaws (bandits) were in ambush and had killed many people and warned us not to pass through Dhedheessaa valley at night time. Obbo Baayisaa told my husband that the prayer that he often prayed was not enough, but this time, he needed to stand on one foot and pray fervently all night long for our safety.

One time at Aira School, the teachers prepared a program for students' educational entertainment and debate at the end of the school year. This was done annually and had become a tradition. At the end of every school year, the school invited family members, officials, and the judges in the community.

The topic of the debate was about the coming of the missionaries to our country. The debate was on whether the coming of the missionaries was good or bad for our country. One group was led by Dr. Nagassoo Gadaadaa, and the other by Obbo Tsegayee Namarraa. Nagassoo's group, which debated that the coming of the missionaries to our country was beneficial and gave their reasons. Tsegaye's group debated against the coming of the missionaries to the country and gave their reasons.

At the end of the debate, the judges (those who chaired the debate) gave their verdict on the bases of the strength of arguments on both sides. Finally, the judges announced that Tsegaye's group has won the debate.

After the debate was over, the school director asked the audience for comments. While the judge (government official) and the other officials were listening, my husband raised his hand and voiced his opinion opposing the verdict of the judges of the debate.

He said, "Everything I built in the last fifty years, Tsegaye came to Aira to nullify in one night."

So he urged that the verdict be revoked and the entire matter be reexamined. He was factual in his reasoning.

Everybody, including the judge and the other officials, were amazed but also enjoyed the laughter.

One time on his way to the court, he stopped to eat his food under the shade of a tree beside the road. An Orthodox priest, who accused him for starting the Evangelical Church (Lutheran) met him, and my husband shared the food that I prepared for him with his accuser who was taking him to court. The man did not have food with him and was very hungry, and he thanked my husband for the food. They went to the court together and came back to Aira together.

Similar things happened often. My husband ate with and lived his life with his opponents, the Orthodox Church clergy and government officials, without holding grudges against them. We all laughed, talked, and joked about it all the time. For us, this was a Christian way of life expected from us that we share life with all humankind.

One time, there was a revival conference in Dambii Dolloo to which my husband was invited as one of the conference preachers. Unfortunately, my husband had an appointment at the court on that very day. So my husband decided to send Luba Ashanaa Nagaadee to Dambii Dolloo to cover for him.

At one occasion, my husband went to Naqamtee to see to it that the Christians who were in prison were released. Luba Gidaadaa's teaching at the conference was advice to the pastors and the believers, especially to the pastors, not to drink alcoholic beverages so that they could have a clear mind to be able to preach the gospel. Luba Ashanaa came back from Dambii Dolloo and told my husband what Luba Gidaadaa taught and asked my husband to do the same in teaching the pastors and the congregations.

All the people whom we taught and helped to follow Christ started complaining to my husband. My husband quickly sent back Luba Ashanaa Negaadee to Luba Gidadaa to review his teaching by telling the pastors not to drink and the people may drink with the warning of limitation not to get drunk. His quotation from the Bible was **"Stop drinking only water. And use a little wine because of your stomach and your frequent illnesses" (1 Timothy 5:23).**

My husband started strictly teaching the people to know about life itself. Alcohol is not allowed at any time for a Christian life, but it is good to know what is good and bad for our lives.

20

RETIREMENT

My husband retired in the early 1980s after giving over seventy years of service. He worked as an organizer, director, teacher, counselor, pastor, and president for twenty-five years. His successor as the president of western synod was Pastor Tasgara Hirpo. At his retirement, the western synod gave him one Holy Bible as appreciation for his service, and he received it with grace.

After his retirement, the Mekane Yesus Church president and a couple of pastors came from Finfinnee to Aira for the opening celebration of our hostel that was built by the German Hermannsburg Mission. My husband was supposed to cut the ribbon that day, but he was sick in bed, and they came to our little home and gave him a karat of gold before they returned to Finfinnee. They told him that it was part of his retirement gift.

My husband was thankful for the gift but asked, "Since you came all the way to celebrate the opening of this hostel, did you all put some money toward the growth of the new hostel?"

They replied, "No."

The three of them were surprised and embarrassed by his question.

He advised them to support the hostel in the future. It seemed like my husband knew what would take place in the future. Sure enough, nobody remembered to give to the hostel, and sadly enough, the hostel was closed after his death.

People around us were surprised when they found out about his retirement gifts and asked him how he felt about receiving them.

He replied, "A gift is a gift."

Some of our close friends, and specifically, Obbo Tasfaayee Darasuu, laughed and told them, "The reward of this pastor is from his God alone, not from the church or the people he served."

Obbo Tasfaayee Darasuu said, "We did not expect this reward from the synod, but it should have been something that we all enjoy looking at and call after his name and that lasts long to tell the story of this wise man for the future generations."

Even if people around him complained about the gift, my husband never complained about anything but thanked his Creator in everything. He never bragged about himself. That was the man I knew.

About three years before his death, a few European ambassadors came to Aira with the German embassy officials for celebration of the fiftieth anniversary of the arrival of the German Hermannsburg Mission in Aira, a fulfillment of Louis Harms's dreams of many years.

After the celebration was over, the German officials came to our home to appreciate my husband for his accomplishments by saying that the dream of Louis Harms got its fulfillment by the efforts of Daffa and Wassmann, and that the job was well done.

My husband was not feeling well enough to attend the event, but his reply to the German consulate was that the job he did was done by the grace of God. He noted that it was the duty that God had entrusted to him, and he accepted it with joy.

I have never considered his retirement to be a real retirement because he worked day and night until a couple of years before his death. One of the reasons was that when the Durg took over the government, the younger generation joined the new government and caused a lot of trouble for our churches and disrupted many of the regular programs of the church. The majority of the youngsters in the area went along in supporting the new government.

The people were totally changed, closed churches in our area, and we had to go underground to get together and worship. We had

After retirement with Mr. Emmanuel Abraham in front of Aira Hospital

to plead with the government to open our churches for us so that we could have our worship services. We went through a lot of trouble in those days.

The young pastors were scared of preaching, baptizing, and doing any of their pastoral duties. They sent word to my husband to do the job. None of them came out of their house to preach. If they were seen going to church, they would be arrested.

But nobody arrested my husband because they had great respect for him and because of his many years of service for the community and his old age. They knew he had done so many good things for them and their fathers at one time or another. That's the reason the area pastors asked my husband to go out and do the jobs for them.

My husband never reminded them that he was retired and never said no to any one of them. He continued to work until he turned eighty-eight. He slowly cut back after his body started to weaken. At the same time, he was writing books. He wrote about twenty-seven books, some of which are already printed and in use at universities. He died at the age of ninety-two.

After his retirement, my husband went to the hospital every single morning to pray for the doctors, nurses, hospital workers, and the sick until he could no longer walk. He visited all the patients individually and prayed for them. This was his daily routine throughout his retirement period.

Dr. Doorenbos told him that he was a "spiritual doctor, while he was a physical doctor." He took this to heart, and he did his part until a year before his death. When he visited the children in the hospital, the nurses gathered them all in one place for him to teach them the Bible verses and prayer. After that, he played with them and told them varieties of stories to make them laugh. They all call him Grandpa, "Akkakaa." The children could not wait until he got there every morning. They would run up to him and give him a hug and tell him that they were ready to hear some more children's stories and play fun games.

The doctors told us not to let him go anywhere by himself, but he refused to let anybody follow him. He always thought that he was strong enough to take care of himself.

One morning, a man saw him walking to the hospital alone and asked him why he came out by himself without somebody accompanying him to help him if he fell.

My husband answered him, "No one will stop me from going out. Even if I fall, wouldn't you pick me up?"

The man answered him that he would.

Then my husband said to him, "Fine, then all of these areas are full of people, and they see me walking and they will not leave me on the ground but pick me up."

The man was amazed and said, "True, nobody will pass you."

We used to tell him not to go far from home by himself, but later on, he himself decided on his own to stop walking by himself just nine months before his death.

Rev. Manfred Zach & Rev. Daffa meeting with Christian friends.

One of our missionary friends, who worked tirelessly with my husband and retired in Germany, wrote us a letter, saying, "Pastor Daffa, our synod need to check on us more often."

My husband was sad to hear that and said that it was not fair, especially to all missionaries who worked throughout their lives to help us grow in our Christian life. They had the choice of raising their children in comfort in their own country at a European standard, but they chose instead to help us out in our situation. I thank the Lord and appreciate the missionaries for what they did for us.

I concluded from the start, as I have discussed earlier, that we could not live on the income we were getting from the church to cover the expenses to carry out our work of spreading the gospel and to carry on all the activities we were intending to do to help our society. We were not rich by our country's standard, but we toiled and saved some money over the years to buy a plot of land to build our house and have our own coffee plantation on our land. We had a coffee plantation, where I labored for years. From our coffee plantation, we got just enough to meet our needs and the needs of our children as they were growing up.

We also had a large fruit garden around our house for which I was also responsible. We got some income from that. As Christians, we did what we believed was appropriate. We had hoped that we would be getting just enough income from all these for our retirement without expecting help from our children or anyone else.

Unfortunately, things did not work out as we have planned because of the change of government. The Communist regime of Mengistu Hailemariam took power in 1974 by overthrowing Haile Selassei's government and with it the entire feudal system in Ethiopia. This paved the way for nationalizing properties, including land. Our coffee plantation and our land were nationalized.

Though our people were relieved of serfdom temporarily, it did not bring prosperity to them. Things were out of control. The situation was chaotic, and some people lost their lives in addition to their properties. People were still in deadening poverty. The country generally remained poor. But the regime took everything it could and labeled the people as corrupt, noncorrupt, abusive, and nonabusive. The upper-class people were all labeled as corrupt if they had some kind of property and were well-to-do.

To make matters worse for us, one of our children became a political prisoner in Finfinnee for eleven years, as mentioned earlier, during the Durge regime, and my sister Elizabeth Karorsa fled to the United States of America for political reasons.

When God closes one door, He opens another. We turned to our children and my sister Elizabeth, who were abroad, to help us financially at that time. I also worked hard on my handcrafts.

My husband retired in 1980 with a salary of 200 birr a month, an amount that is equivalent to less than $10 and not enough to live on at that time. However, we had never depended on the money we were getting as a salary from the church or the synod in the first place. Had it not been for help from our children, we could not have survived on 200 birr a month. We thank our Lord for giving us a handful of blessed children in addition to my talents of handcrafts.

All our children from America and Germany poured their hearts out and their money out on us in order for us to survive for several years. After my husband retired, he became sick and required special treatment and medications. My children would send him medicine and all the expensive medical kits—not available in Ethiopia—monthly or every other month, which he used regularly without stopping for over fifteen years.

Some of our children could not come to see us for political reasons, but Hanna, Tsion, and Deribe would take turns every year or every other year to come and visit us and do all the necessary things that we both needed. Our children not only supported us but also supported many of our extended family members and friends by paying for their school fees, hospital bills, and clothing.

Mathew 25:35 says, "For I was hungry and you gave me something to eat, I was thirsty and you gave me something to drink, I was a stranger and you invited me in, I needed clothes and you clothed me, I was sick and you looked after me, I was in prison and you came to visit me." We never expected any handouts from anybody, but our God arranged things for us the way He wanted, and He met all our needs according to His will, and prepared us even before we started our journey together.

Even after our retirement, as I mentioned earlier we continue giving a helping hands. Thus, we decided to take over the raising of my late brother's children. My only brother, Faajjii Karorsaa, passed away during his children's adolescent years. His firstborn son,

Berhanu, died also and had no kids. Ruth got married and had six children. His last son, Dawit Faajjii, got married. He had seven children of his own and died of malaria at a young age.

We ended up raising them all. Their names are Ejerso, Lamesa, Margee, Qananie Bontuu, Rommee, and Obsee. We consider them all to be our own grandchildren. Raising these children at our old age was not easy, but it was a joy having them around and them calling us grandma (Akko) and grandpa (Akaakaa).

Our children supported them by paying their school fees and clothing them. They also supported the extended family around us, especially Ejersoo and Lamessaa, who graduated from college. Now they are professionals, and the rest of them are successful in their fields. Some of them are already married and have their own families. It is a blessing watching them grow and have their own families.

My husband was naturally a storyteller, and he used his time teaching them old stories of the family and Oromo culture. Every evening was the kids' fiction storytelling time. It was like a fantasy watching the children sitting by him and listening to his teaching them the children's stories, animal stories, and a variety of cultural games. Their joyful time was wintertime, when all the kids got together and made coffee with roasted fresh corn and created their own joyful evening playtime with their grandfather. This part was never skipped, and I think my husband left a good lesson for all of them that they can use to teach their own children.

When my husband passed away, Shaashituu and Taayyee, Amentee's children, Marriaa and Asfaw's children, and the entire Aira community were with him in Aira hospital. Ejersoo, Lamessaa, Jootee, and Caalaa took turns holding his hand to pray for him.

But the call of God came and took him away from them. They were in the hospital from Sunday, February 25, 2002, to the last day of his life on February 28, 2002.

Kanatu at Rev. Daffa's grave in 2002

We love the Aira community dearly, and I hope that they kept the good memory of their grandfather and will use the lessons they learned from him at the last stages of his life.

21

LIFE AFTER THE DEPARTURE OF MY HUSBAND

I truly believe that God in His creative way can bring His goodness out of our pain. I also believe that we have to be willing to see the good that comes our way. I am convinced that even the most tragic loss can be turned into good if we allow it to be.

One of the astonishing things that cannot be changed in life after death is that the sun continues to rise and set. Life goes on, and people will go about their business as though no one's world has been shaken to the core.

In everyone's life, God has a way of healing, and He is there to hold and comfort those who grieve. Death is always new and a surprise to humankind, but for Christ's followers, it is a call to home, to everlasting life. **"To those who by persistence in doing good seek glory, honor and immortality, He will give eternal life" (Romans 2:7).**

When our Lord comes, He will make sure

Kanatu standing by Rev Daffa's grave in 2003

that everyone receives the knowledge of God's plan, which offers eternal life to all who believe and obey Him. We know and believe that someday we will get together at our Lord's loving home. We are always in His care in this life and beyond.

Starting a new chapter of my life was quite a challenge to me, but by the grace of God, I managed and believed that God wouldn't give me what I couldn't handle, for He is and will always be there in our lives.

One year after my husband's death, in 2003, life in Aira came to an end because my children wanted me to move to Finfinnee until I could get my visa to the United States. The main reason for my move to the United States was to be close to my children, and also watch my grandchildren grow. At the time, two of our children lived in Germany, one in Finfinnee, and the other five lived in the United States.

Our children did everything possible to keep me comfortable in Finfinnee for three years while my visa to the United States was being processed. It was very difficult at that time for an Ethiopian to get a visa to the USA.

After three years in Finfinnee, I finally got my visa at the end of June 2005. My children sent my daughter Tsion to come to get me. Now, I am residing with our children in Dallas, Texas. I am grateful to God for giving me a long life to reflect on our lives together and enabling me now to tell the story of our journey together.

Kanatu with my daughter Tsion.

Before my children asked me to move to the United States, I had not even thought of leaving our home behind to live far from our community. But no one knows what the future holds. God is the One who planned the way for me before I was born. After I came to the United States, I had plenty of time on my hands, and I continued working on my handcrafts and beading. I enjoy reading my Bible and doing a variety of handcrafts. I have never spent the day without working on my handcrafts.

I am so happy that He kept me in good health to accomplish all that I have enjoyed doing in my life. I am a creative and innovative artist who honors God with my handcrafts daily, constantly producing new variations and seeing improvement on my products.

I never get tired of working on my handcrafts. It gives me satisfaction and great joy when I create new designs that turn out to be perfect.

Grandchildren

The Reminiscence of Our Lives In My Own Words

I am now enjoying life with my children and grandchildren. It is a joy of my life and blessing to watch them grow. At this time, I am limited in my movement, and I cannot go around as I wish. Life in the United States does not allow me to do as much by myself as I used to do when I was in my homeland. In my country, I had a lot of neighbors to visit. The hospital and the church were close to our home, and I never spent a day without working in my garden or without people around me. Now, I have to wait for the weekends for my children to get together to enjoy them. Three of my children live in Dallas, Texas, and two of them live in different states and come to Dallas to visit me every now and then.

We share the old stories and bring up the memories that we have in our hearts and cherish the moments. Saturday afternoons, my son Saamu'el comes over, our girls make coffee and a variety of food, and we sit around to enjoy the day. Late in the evenings, just like back home, we prepare ourselves for Sunday to go to church and enjoy the day as well. I am counting my blessings each day of my life.

22

ACCOMPLISHMENTS

My husband's trip to a European country was an eye opener for his vision of christian life. It introduced him to his christian friends abroad. What he had learnt, and the faith he had developed from Rev. Dietrich Wassmann and from the Swedish pastors came to light. He was focused and had faith that he can spread the word of God and love to wherever he can go. His aim from this journey was to gain more knowledge of christian life and bring it back to our country and educated our people. He was determined towards the growth of his peoples spiritually, educationally and economically. To create a network or build international relations between the European and our country within the church so that our people will live in a way of the civilized country. The German Hermansburg mission welcomed him and he visited so many Scandinavian countries to make speech or preach. Rev. Wassmann had introduced my husband before his arrival and they knew what to expect from him. In my mind both my husband and the missionary profited from each other. The benefit of the missionaries was to hear the product of their effort done outside of their country of introducing the gospel to the people of the country. The benefit of my husband was to gain more knowledge for himself and bring spiritual education to his people. On this project he did not only work on Spiritual workshops but schools and hospitals. Because of his many speeches he made wherever he went he convinced them to help him build so many churches, schools and hospitals in our country. They increased the number of missionaries, the number of teachers, doctors and nurses. The Oromo people benefited a lot from his work for many years and are still benefiting from it as their living standards are improving through education he kindled. As a result, so many doctors and nurses and students with different kinds of degrees were produced in so many fields benefiting not only the Oromo people but the whole country. The network of his work was expanded throughout the international christians and also well established in our country.

We both gave our lives to God to guide our people to eternal life. My husband's focus was more on congregations, schools, and the community at large. I believe God had a purpose for me when He laid the foundation of my married life of sixty-seven years with my husband. After he served the church for a total of over seventy years as a pastor and twenty-five years as president of the western synod, he went to His loving God on February 28, 2002 at age ninety-two.

"However, I consider my life worth nothing to me, if only I may finish the race and complete the task the Lord Jesus has given me—the task of testifying the gospel of God's grace" (Acts 20:24).

I supported my husband in all possible ways until the last day of his life. In the course of our lives together, we have come to know that the Lord does not give us rules, but He makes His standard very clear. If our relationship with Him is that of love, we do what He says without hesitation. We quickly recognized that Jesus did not force us to obey Him, but we were committed to do so. Obedience leads to spiritual destiny.

Every hope and dream of humankind will be fulfilled in accordance to the will of God. But one of the greatest difficulties in life is the difficulty of waiting on God. When we patiently wait for the time of God, He accomplishes His purpose in our lives at His own time.

I believe our Lord Jesus Christ has been pleased in what He has done through us. God placed us where we were because that was the place we could be of use to Him. Our minds are the gifts of God to us. They are given to us to be used for His purpose. It is important that we should not lose sight of His gift.

My husband was totally satisfied with what he did in his life for his people and God. That is what kept me in good spirit and gave me strength. I am overwhelmingly thankful to God with what He has accomplished in our lifetime. All the work we did together to accomplish the will of Christ Jesus were done because He chose us at the right time for His work. We testify that He is Lord and Savior of our souls who called us so that those who have not come to know Jesus Christ as Lord and Savior may come to know Him and be saved.

God enabled us to see our dreams come true and helped us experience life in Jesus Christ to the fullest. We believe we performed well and have confidence that our lives were well spent raising our children, serving the congregations, and putting our community in a better position. We secured a wealth of wisdom to share, and we humbly provided pieces of advice and left a good example for the young generation.

"Blessed is the man who finds wisdom, the man who gains understanding" (Proverbs 3:13).

It was a privilege and an opportunity that God allowed us to be useful and productive in the service of our community. Truly, age is beautiful and delightful. Both of us wanted to go with patience knowing that God would go before us and prepare a place for us. Our yesterday is simply holding the memory of our past. We have today at hand to enjoy the moment. We dream about tomorrow and keep it all in our hearts as long as we live. Jesus Christ is the same yesterday, today, and for ages to come.

We cherish the memory of our leadership, teaching the Word of God, and reflect on the result of our effort. We wanted every human being to have a chance to know Him and live according to the principles of Christian life that Christ Jesus desires. Our delightful lives with God are the memory of yesterday, and He allowed that memory to turn into a ministry of spiritual growth for our future. All that we did was for the glory of God. That was the service we gave to our God who called both of us to serve Him, and He directed us on the road to eternal life.

"I have finished the work which you have given me to do" (John 17:4). Our life of service to God is ***"My Thank You"*** to Him. He is our wonderful Savior!

23
LETTERS AND POEMS FROM OUR CHILDREN

THE DAFFA FAMILY

The Reminiscence of Our Lives
In My Own Words

Gratitude and Appreciation

We know that both of you have been there for us ever since we were born. We love you and have great respect for you, Mom and Dad. We are not sure if you know how much we appreciate everything you have done for us, though. Both of you are our personal role models. We look up to both of you all the time, even when you do not realize it. Your spirit and memory live in us and whisper in our ears forever.

You have been our guides in the world from our first tentative, unsure steps, both as infants and as young children attending schools at different places and levels. When our legs felt like they would collapse under us at any moment, we could call either of you and know you would be there to catch us before we hit the ground.

No matter where we had been or how far away we were located, in provinces or countries, nothing could separate us from both of you. We knew you were always there for us. You do not know how much we appreciate your constant concern and unconditional love. Even though we did not get a chance to talk to you or write to you every day, we constantly think of you. Our love is unconditional for both of you then, now, and forever.

Ababba (Father)!

To other people, you are one person, but to us, you are the world! You have been a strong rock for us to lean on!

You gave us strength with your warm, quiet nature. You heard us asking you endless, unanswerable, and sometimes even hard questions. We would fight and scream at each other for no reason, and you would absorb and swallow it all without complaint. Then you would find the right words at the right time to respond to our random questions, to guide us on our way.

You showed and told us that we could and would handle the obstacles in front of us, and you would calm us down. You also encouraged us to think of alternative viewpoints so that we could learn how to lean on God when we face challenges in our lives. Thank you for your patience and thoughtful guidance as a wonderful father and wise pastor to us.

You traveled a lot on foot and by mule to spread the saving gospel of Jesus Christ. When we were young, we did not get a chance to play with you as much as other children did with their fathers. We did not understand how hard you were working, but still, when you came home from your journeys, we expected you to play with us, and you never complained or lost the will to do so.

As one of the best fathers, you wanted to make us happy by checking our schoolwork and teaching us the Word of God, as well as cultural and spiritual songs and different games that you learned from your father and mother.

We respected and valued that you preferred to fulfill God's call. You paved the way for the young and old. You did not show any partiality between humankind created by God; all were equal and valuable to you. You did your best to lead your people to the land of promise, like Moses of the Old Testament. You fought a good fight for the captives and freed them from prison; you stood by the side of the helpless during those dark days. We are grateful to God for giving us such a great and wise father like you.

You gave us the joy and love of your heart. You showed us how to be patient, honest, strong, sincere, kind, loving, and hard-working. You taught us how to fight for human rights and not to take any step out of fear of a man but to stand still and hear the truth of God. You showed us how we should act and how we should treat others. You were a teacher, a mentor, and a messenger of God to us.

You executed your duty that you accepted from God perfectly and the people whose lives you touched will never forget what you planted in them. You are a treasure of our lives forever. Never forget that no matter how old we are today, we always remain your offspring. We love you dearly and unconditionally, ABABBA!

The Reminiscence of Our Lives In My Own Words

A father ahead of his time,
Then, God's call reached you to divine!
Along with God's gift of knowledge,
You accepted the call full of courage!

You led your children and people on God's way,
You taught all how to live and obey!
Full of determination and guidance,
You never looked back but marched forward in confidence!

You poured your heart to please your Creator,
You never allowed any distractions from your prayer.
Ahead of yourself you put your only God,
You gave your heart and faith for Him to guide!

God gave you Mamma to start a new life
He knew His Word needs focus laser-like.
So, you were united in marriage,
When both of you were at a very young age.
You were blessed with nine children,
And a handful grandchildren.

God sent Wassmann to start the Mission,
And you spread the Word without commission,
God planted in you the sense of passion,
And you carried your duty with great compassion.

He knew your heart was full of wisdom,
He guided you to the road of the Kingdom.
Your dreams and wishes came through as He planned,
He gave you strength through the great command.

He guided you through all the work to design,
You built hospitals, churches, and schools in line.
You never looked back and never complained,
You lifted your eyes to heaven towards Christ who reigns.

Rev. Daffa Jammo and I

You walked barefoot in rain, sun, day and night,
To fulfill your promise so that everything would be all right.

God picked you to be his own vessel,
Therefore, He planted you where He can level.
You were ready to work as you heard His call,
His command was clear and you took up the role,

You helped your people to see God's green pasture,
That gave your Creator the greatest pleasure!
Nothing left behind for you was unsatisfied,
Nothing left from your work that wasn't fulfilled!

We saw and heard you teaching from God's Holy Word
And to all you were truly a gentle guard,
Nothing kept you from reaching the Promised Land.
No matter the hour; whatever the need,
You traveled barefoot to complete the work indeed!

Always ready and willing to share,
A comforting thought and smile with care.
When rain and storms replaced the sunny weather,
You paved the road so all was clear,
And you invited folks to the Word in order for them to hear.

Protected your flock from all snares,
Attended to all your people's cares.
Dedicated to your people to give it all,
So that they tenderly listened to the Spirit's call.

We thought of you every moment and every hour,
We miss you now more than ever before,
We know that you are under God's power.

Your gentle nature carried you to your destination,
Your daily effort and faithful devotion,
Captured your dreams with great jubilation.
At your leisure He lifted you up,
And now you are at the **mountaintop**!

As much as you can, you obeyed the Master's commands,
You finished your race with great demands,
Now you rest from all your labor in God's comforting hands!
We know that your job was done well when you were alive,
And now, you rest in peace until we meet on the other side of life!

Mamma (Mother)!

You have always been there in so many ways for us. You listen to our worries, hear our complaints, watch us strive to find our path, and see us learn. You reassure us that all will be well and gave us advice, bring us back when we wander, nudge, and guide us in the right direction, then stand back and watch us grow.

We have a bond that only mothers and children can share. You understood each one of us because you loved us. Whenever something bad happened, we ran to you first to seek a solution. We know how to love, laugh, cry tears of joy, and feel sad on bad days.

You encourage us every day, and you constantly remind us that we are better than or equal to anyone else. You prepared us to stand for our rights as well as the rights of others and encouraged us to speak up to protect whoever was in need.

We learned from you how to handle different situations in life. You taught us many of our cultural and religious values. You showed us what true respect looks like. You exhausted yourself to nurture and raise us to be good citizens. We will forever be grateful for all that you have done for us.

Thank you for being our loving mom and for the blessings you have poured on us ever since we were born. We love you and cherish all the good and bad memories we shared with you. Most importantly, we adore you for helping our father at his old age with his sickness.

You raised his children almost by yourself; you met all his needs when he wrote his books; you stood by him when he planted hundreds of different community churches as well as building hospitals and schools; you were with him in his efforts to cuddle the congregations as needed. You really completed the work you received from God. We thank God for leading you to our father.

> A mother with full of love,
> Whose heart God opened to love,
> He gave you full of talent and wisdom,
> To guide His people to His kingdom.
>
> He guided you to a wise gentleman,
> Having known that you both had something in common.
> What a joyful accommodation,
> For through you His purpose had great jubilation!
>
> He did not leave you with him alone,
> Rather He blessed you with children to be born,
> Who gave you a special bond that sprinkles through years,
> During the events of laughter, worries, smiles, and tears!
>
> With a sense of trust that can't be broken,
> And a depth of love often spoken,
> A lifelong friendship built on sharing,
> Hugs and kisses, warmth and caring,

The Reminiscence of Our Lives In My Own Words

Mother and children their heart as one,
A link that can never be undone,
His aim and plan had not vanished,
For you listen to His Word to be nourished!

You were a stepping stone for your community,
You worked so hard for humanity,
The task you took up was not easy to bear,
You managed to accomplish the promise with others to share,
While He gently guided you with love and care!

Your work and effort shines over the mountaintop,
You never give in and never give up,
For the poor and needy always firmly you stood up,
As He planned for you to be His vessel cup.

Your people look at you as a wise woman,
The love of your heart is already woven,
Something special to you had already been given,
In your heart His Word is firmly written.

You did your part to educate your people,
You led all to hear the Gospel,
You surely became one of His disciples.
You stood by our father until his last day,
A strong and faithful wife is all we can say,
Blessings from above be with you, we pray!

Your sacrifices and unselfishness did not go unnoticed,
Truly your work and goals are well accomplished,
Job well done, Mamma, and you're always blessed!

Mamma's talent should be told,
We cannot put it on hold,
From a little memory in our mind that we stored!

Rev. Daffa Jammo and I

A multitalented woman,
Rarely found in the nature of a human,
To you, all knowledge was given,
Your God showered on you from heaven.

Blessed with the skill of handcrafting,
Who taught the village how to bead, crochet, knit, and plant,
You offered all that you have without any greed,
And you enjoy granting, that was your gift indeed.

The flowers and gardens around our home that used to bloom,
How beautiful they looked, and they were really groomed,
The house was kept clean in each and every room.

The wind never stopped blowing from left to right,
To spread the smell of fruits and flowers and ready to invite,
That was the sign for neighbors to share and delight.

Butterflies with beautiful colors keep on flying,
And the hummingbirds were still vying,
What a joyful melody to hear while on the beds we were lying,
Along with the honeybees roaring in the air, it was exciting,
All other creatures were dancing and singing,
Those sounds never left us, in our ears they're still ringing.

When we looked at our garden, we felt a sense of pride,
Its medium size or even comparatively large and wide,
It rather looked like a lovely room if it weren't just outside.
It was rewarding to us—it felt like we won a prize.

We still cherish the harmony of nature,
Growing while watching different cultures,
That made us wonder about the power of our Creator.

At that time, we felt like we were in the Garden of Eden,
We enjoyed our small world that we were given,

The Reminiscence of Our Lives In My Own Words

And we praised the Lord for blessing us on earth and in Heaven.

Surely neighbors were invited from corner to corner,
You didn't feel like you were the only owner,
Rather, you welcomed all with true and full honor!

As the neighbors at our home were on board,
You pulled your Bible from the shelf to teach the Word,
In order to read the whole story of the Lord
That was the time to share with all what was well stored.

You loved to share your life, and that was your linkage,
You carried the seedling around the village,
For your neighborhood it was a big privilege,
To imprint and leave it there as a solid and great image.

When father traveled, you pack the BREAD to break,
Along with the fruits for the people to take.
Fruits for physical, the Word for spiritual,
How did you plan ahead to make that so mutual?
Father was satisfied with feeding all as usual,
That was your deep value, and it became to all a ritual.

You also used to pack a variety of patterns,
For those who left for a far distance, you created a lantern,
And you are ready to share from the knowledge you earned,
You attached your design with a needle and yarn for the women to learn.
Your design was packed and sent as far as Germany,
You did not want to keep it to your people only,
Amazing, Father and Pastor Harms transported for you those designs mostly.

After you reached Dallas, you became transmittal,
And the ELCA women group found you committal,
You made nice, warm socks for Parkland Hospital,

To help the cancer patients, to you it was a solid vital.
Wow, your hand was starched from home to across the ocean,
It was done very well, for that was your notion.

When father came from work anytime of the day,
If he got a chance to come home by the way,
Our hearts were filled with joy as he watched us play.
He enjoyed watching us running after the butterflies,
Surely, he watched the little ones close to his eyes,
And got a moment to teach us through some cultural exercise.

Remember you made us work in the house or in a garden,
Or to abuse the privilege of child and parenthood bargain,
Even in the unfriendly weather and wetness of the rain,
You wanted us to learn and help while you picked all the grain,
How it was not fun to work hard, but it was a pain,
Your plan was perfect for the knowledge we gained.

What a mixture of life that we lived in,
With the multitalents of work that was bestowed within
We pray to keep the memory in our hearts,
We praise the Lord who created you both so smart.

We wanted to share a bit from our own childhood memory,
For sure it is a lot to tell, but we did not keep the whole summary,
What we saw and kept in our little minds without sensory,
Both of your lives are so full of glory,
And this is just a small part of your story,
To God now and forever be the glory.

The most beautiful thing for any human being is to see their parents smiling and knowing that you are the reason behind that smile and happiness.

Both of you have helped in transforming us into kind of human beings we are today. We could not have become who we are without either of you. You introduced us to God from day 1 of our lives but never pressured us; you only guided us. You allowed and taught us to know, understand, and love God. We cannot imagine a world without Him.

Thank you for giving us the best of gift you could ever give us: our education and our confidence. You pushed us to be the best we could be, encouraged us to aim high, picked us up when we fell, and supported us the entire way. Both of you are the best parents we could ever ask for, and we are forever grateful that we can call you mom and dad.

We love you both and are proud to tell the outshining story of your lives to our children as well as to the young generation to come. Both of you are God's gift to us.

All glory to God for giving us both of you as our parents!

24

NOTES FROM OUR GODCHILDREN DR. BICHAKA FAYISSA AND MS. ASTER BATO

What I Remember of Mamma Kanatu Karorsa and Pastor Daffa Jammo

Dr. Bichaka Fayissa

My name is Bichaka Fayissa, professor in the Department of Economics and Finance, Middle Tennessee State University, Murfreesboro, Tennessee. This short essay about Mamma Kanatu Karorsa and Pastor Daffa Jammo is based on some of my childhood recollections, growing up in Aira Wollaga over fifty years ago. It is also based on my readings of a few anecdotal writings about Mamma Kanatu Karorsa and Pastor Daffa Jammo, the first family of the Aira Lutheran Church.

The Reminiscence of Our Lives In My Own Words

Mamma Kanatu was born and raised in Dembi Dollo by American missionaries, while Pastor Daffa was born in the small village of Qannawo located between Gimbi and Dembi Dollo, Wollaga.

At a young age, Pastor Daffa moved to Aira, where he grew up as a great entrepreneur making raincoats, raising chickens and goats for money, getting training, and working in many different roles with the German missionaries, especially with Pastor Wassmann, who taught him the German language, while he taught Pastor Wassmann the Oromo language. Together, Pastor Daffa and Pastor Wassmann wrote an Oromo-German dictionary to be used for spreading the Gospel in Aira and surrounding areas.

During the Italian occupation of Ethiopia in the mid-1930s, Pastor Wassmann was forced to move his wife and children to Gambella in order to send them back to Germany via Sudan. On his return back to Aira, Pastor Wassmann spent a night in Dembi Dollo at the American mission compound, where he saw Mamma Kanatu Karorsa, who was a devout Christian girl of fifteen years of age then, being raised in the mission compound.

Pastor Wassmann remembered that his coworker Pastor Daffa Jammo was single at age twenty-five and suggested that the orphan girl be given in marriage to the young priest. Pastor Wassmann also told them that he was going to give Pastor Daffa the responsibility of caring for the Aira mission compound in his absence during the Italian occupation.

The American and German missionaries agreed to this marriage between Mamma Kanatu and Pastor Daffa in January 1936, marking the first Christian wedding ceremony at the Aira church. The couple was blessed with eight surviving children, including Samuel, Paulos, Girma, Hanna, Abby, Daniel, Tsion, and Deribe (source: https://dacb.org/stories/ethiopia/daffa-jammo/).

I will make an effort to share what I can remember about Mamma Kanatu's role of raising her own children and caring for other children of her neighbors, of whom I am one. Actually, I am more than just a neighborhood child to the Daffa family in the sense that Mamma Kanatu is my godmother and Pastor Daffa was my godfather. Mamma Kanatu always reminded me of the sleepless nights she had to endure weaning me from breast-eeding on the east side of the Baqal River, where the family lived and where the old church was located in Walgoo, Aira. She told me that every day, I used to wake up at night and cry for my mother, calling her Negussie, Negussie.

After the Daffa family moved to Lalo Aira, I used to spend many hours daily with the Daffa family. Because my father passed away when I was at a tender age, I looked up to Mamma Kanatu and Pastor Daffa as my adopting parents. I also looked up to their children not only as my brothers and sisters but also as my role models.

The Daffa family placed a priority on the education of their own children and adopted children. They encouraged us to focus on education and celebrated our success. I tried to emulate their focus on education, which sparked in me the spirit of competition and the desire to succeed to escape poverty.

During my elementary years in Aira, Mamma Kanatu and Pastor Daffa also instilled in young boys and girls of Lalo Aira the value of community service by encouraging us to use our school break to help the community by building bridges and assisting the elderly with farming activities. This idea of getting involved in community affairs culminated in the formation of a community service committee known as the "Wayyessaa" Committee under the able leadership of the late brother Dr. Paulos Daffa. *Wayyessaa* literally means "improving, or making the conditions of the community better."

Some of the boys who participated in the committee included Paulos and Girma Daffa, Bichaka Fayissa, Obbo Bantii Dhufeeraa, Elias Nagassa, Olanii Hommaa, Marga Fite, Endaalu Lamu, Ittanaa Galataa, Daniel Daffa, Yosef Chibssaa, Negesse Kidaanee, Danile Tessemaa, Olqabaa Tessemaa, Temesgen Gudataa, Negese Lamu, and others.

Some of the girls who participated in Wayyessaa by cooking and feeding the participants who helped in the construction of bridges, shelter, and the helping the elderly on their farm chores included Aster Bato, Makadash Grangne, Hanna Daffa, Abby Daffa, Adde Zenebetch Darassu, and Djalate Chibsa, Mulunesh and Saraa Jorgo, and others.

In order to operate in different communities outside of the Lalo Aira proper, or jurisdiction, the Wayyessaa self-help organization solicited and received permission from various authorities such as Qenyazmatch Darasu Waraabu, Obbo Grangne Roroo, Balambaras Dheeressaa Sibiluu, and others.

Beyond community service, the members of the Wayyessaa self-help organization had not only a grand ambition of building a school in Yabus (flat land area) but also the vision of constructing an Olympic village to hold Olympic sports competition events after they all earned their degrees. Under the expeditionary mind and leadership of our dear brother Dr. Paulos Daffa, whom we dearly miss so much in death, most of the members of the Wayyessaa committee actually visited the site of the proposed Olympic Village, located in the Yabus area.

Such ambitious childhood dreams would not have been possible without the love and nurturing of the family of Mamma Kanatu Karorsa and Pastor Daffa Jammo.

We owe a great debt of gratitude to Mamma Kanatu Karorsa and Pastor Daffa Jammo's entire family for their love and care and for steering us on the right path in our childhood when we needed support most, especially in my case in the absence of my biological father. I admire and respect our oldest brother Obbo Samuel Daffa, who taught me and my sixth-grade classmates Aster Bato, Elias Negassa, Marga Fite, Olani Homma, Degafu Jobire, and others world geography with great enthusiasm and inspiration.

Personally, my upbringing around the Mamma Kanatu and Ababa Daffa family is a vivid illustration of the popular saying "It takes a village to raise a child."

Finally, I will be remiss if I failed to mention that Mamma Kanatu is a towering figure of the family who managed both the internal and external affairs of her family with respect, grace, and distinction. She made her husband, Pastor Daffa, the love of her lifetime, proud. According to Proverbs 18:22, "He who finds a wife finds a good thing and obtains favor from the Lord." Mamma Kanatu is a favor from the Lord to Ababa Daffa. I love her and am most grateful to my godmother Mamma Kanatu.

Memorable Experiences of My Godmother Aster Bato, Godchild

Aster Bato

"A Wife of Noble Character... She is worth far more than rubies. Her husband has full confidence in her and lacks nothing of value... She is clothed with strength and dignity; she can laugh at the days to come. She speaks with wisdom, and faithful instruction is on her tongue. She watches over the affairs of her household... Her children arise and call her blessed; her husband also, and he praises her... Charm is deceptive, and beauty is fleeting, but a woman who fears the Lord is to be praised. Give her the reward she has earned."

(Proverbs 31:10–31)

I am humbled and overwhelmed with joy to be included in my godmother's autobiography. She is a mother of noble character. My godmother Kanatu Karorsa was married to Pastor (*Luba*) Daffa Jammo, a highly educated, respected pastor, and a pioneer of the Lutheran Church in Ethiopia. He traveled to Germany long before traveling abroad common. He spoke fluent German.

My godmother is friendly, compassionate, vibrant and possesses a sense of humor. Although she gave birth to four boys and four girls, she is lively and full of energy and has retained her youthful look to this date.

I admired my godmother's (*Amama*) and her husband's (Ababa's) relationship. They had a mutual respect for each other and considered each other as equals. They walked side by side, unlike most in our culture, in which women walked behind their husbands.

My earliest memory of my godmother was when they lived about ten miles from our house. They had a house with multiple rooms compared to the rest of the villagers. It was a walking distance from the church where our family attended.

When I found out she was my godmother, I walked by myself to visit her. My godmother has always called me "my child" or "*muuchakoo*." She always welcomed me and others. I felt as if I were one of her children. She has a welcoming attitude toward everyone she met and called them "my child" (*muuchako*). She is a great cook and taught her workers to do the same. I enjoyed her delicious cuisine.

A few years later after my first visit, they built a more modern house made of cement walls with multiple rooms close to where my parents lived.

"Good for me!" I exclaimed. "I do not have to travel that long distance anymore."

In 1994, when I visited my birthplace, my godmother invited me and my brother for lunch, so we walked to their house. The food was delicious.

My godmother always wore modern clothes and stood out from the rest of the women in the village. As the scripture states, "She is clothed with strength and dignity; she can laugh at the days to come" (Proverbs 31:25).

Now that we both live in the United States, when I talk with her on the phone, she has still that youthful voice.

I love her sense of humor and wisdom. My godmother (*Amama*) traveled frequently to Finfinee, the capital of Ethiopia, to visit her sister. It is about six hundred miles away from Aira, Wollaga, where we lived. When she returned from her trip, the villagers would ask her, "Did you see our friends in Finfinee?"

Her response was humorous and intriguing" "Finfinee is not (*gaba jimataa*) a Friday marketplace."

What a wise woman! I heard her say it more than sixty years ago. Nowadays, if people ask me if I have seen their friends, I always tell them my godmother's story.

I am grateful and I thank God that my parents chose *Amama* to be my godmother. She is a woman of God who walks by faith and a model for all Christian wives. She has retained her youthful look and remained strong even in the most trying times.

25

NOTE FROM DR. HARVEY DOORENBOS

Dear Daffa children,

Dr. Doorenbos with family

Margaret and I arrived in Aira in November 1977 (GC) and in a very few days met the distinguished first pastor of the Aira church. What a pleasure it was to get to know Luba Daffa and that he had shepherded the early Christian converts through the days of persecution during the Italian occupation.

At this time in Ethiopian history, he was a stabilizing force during the atheistic, Communistic reign of the Derg. I remember sitting with others while he reviewed some of the protection God had given to the church during that first persecution and assuring those of us listening that God would again protect His flock during this hard time.

The Reminiscence of Our Lives
In My Own Words

We were honored several times to put our feet under the table in Luba Daffa and Haadha Samuel's home to enjoy Budeena and Ettoo Hindanqoo meal. I have a good picture of a time when they returned the honor of a visit to our home. They told us about the early German missionaries, including some of the humorous stories of language mistakes that us foreigners could make in trying to talk Oromo.

I still laugh about the advice a doctor gave to the father of a poorly nourished child that he should feed his child "two grandfathers" every day. She meant *eggs* but mispronounced the word. Politely the father answered he would do just that.

When our son, Dirk, died suddenly in America and we could not go home for his funeral, Luba Daffa and Kanatu were a comfort to us in our loss, as were all the other brothers and sisters in Aira. I remember another occasion when Haadha Samuel and one of her daughters rode back to Aira with us from Finfinee. It was during the rainy season when there were many bad potholes in the roads, and to ensure that we would not get stuck in them, the driver drove fast to avoid the car stopping at a bad place. We were almost home, but I crashed through one mud hole that made the vehicle to jump, causing the passengers in the back seat to crash their heads on the ceiling of the vehicle. And it was not a small, gentle bump.

"Go on, Doctor, go on, we'll be all right."

Most of our memories are simple, everyday events, but all are fond memories. My work at the hospital and Margaret's work at the school were always supported by the Daffa family. God has rewards for them for being faithful children and servants.

With Christian love and joy,
Harvey Doorenbos

Mrs. Kanatu Karorsa, at age ninety-seven

The Reminiscence of Our Lives
In My Own Words

Rev. Daffa Jammo and Mrs. Kanatu Karorsa